FRANCIS FRITH'S

PORTSMOUTH - A H
CELEBRATION

Dear Pops/Grandad

A trip down memory lane!

With all our love on your birthday

Sam, Olly and Freya xxxx

THE FRANCIS FRITH COLLECTION

www.francisfrith.com

PORTSMOUTH
A HISTORY & CELEBRATION

SARAH QUAIL

THE FRANCIS FRITH COLLECTION

www.francisfrith.com

First published in the United Kingdom in 2005
by The Francis Frith Collection®

Hardback Edition 2005 ISBN 1-84589-215-1
Paperback Edition 2011 ISBN 978-1-84589-599-0

British Library Cataloguing in Publication Data

Portsmouth - A History & Celebration
Sarah Quail

The Francis Frith Collection
Oakley Business Park, Wylye Road,
Dinton, Wiltshire SP3 5EU
Tel: +44 (0) 1722 716 376
Email: info@francisfrith.co.uk
www.francisfrith.com

Printed and bound in England

Front Cover: **PORTSMOUTH, TRAMS AT CLARENCE PIER** ZZZ04520t
(Portsmouth City Museums and Records Service)

Additional modern photographs by Sarah Quail.

Domesday extract used in timeline by kind permission of
Alecto Historical Editions, www.domesdaybook.org
Aerial photographs reproduced under licence from
Simmons Aerofilms Limited.
Historical Ordnance Survey maps reproduced under licence from
Homecheck.co.uk

Every attempt has been made to contact copyright holders of
illustrative material. We will be happy to give full acknowledgement in
future editions for any items not credited. Any information should be
directed to The Francis Frith Collection.

*The colour-tinting in this book is for illustrative purposes only,
and is not intended to be historically accurate*

AS WITH ANY HISTORICAL DATABASE, THE FRANCIS FRITH ARCHIVE
IS CONSTANTLY BEING CORRECTED AND IMPROVED, AND THE
PUBLISHERS WOULD WELCOME INFORMATION ON OMISSIONS OR
INACCURACIES

CONTENTS

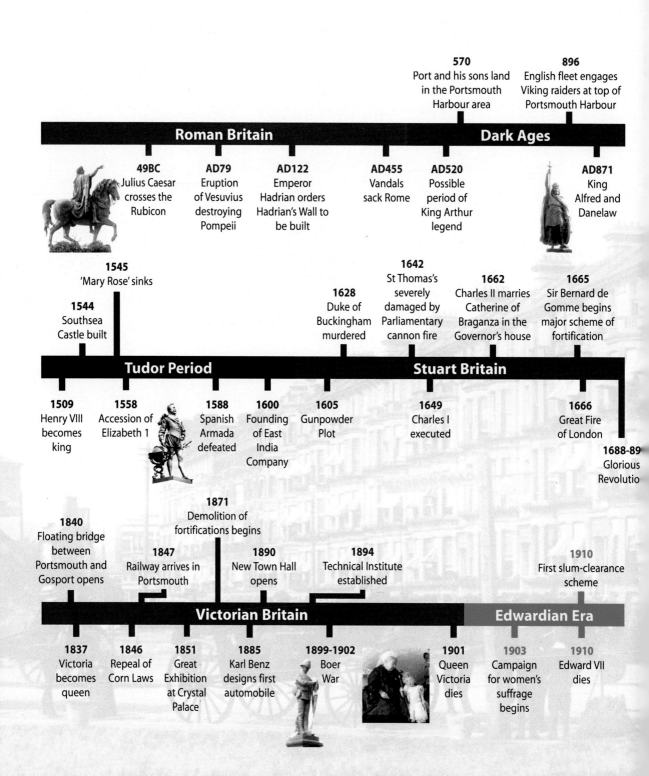

570
Port and his sons land in the Portsmouth Harbour area

896
English fleet engages Viking raiders at top of Portsmouth Harbour

Roman Britain

Dark Ages

49BC
Julius Caesar crosses the Rubicon

AD79
Eruption of Vesuvius destroying Pompeii

AD122
Emperor Hadrian orders Hadrian's Wall to be built

AD455
Vandals sack Rome

AD520
Possible period of King Arthur legend

AD871
King Alfred and Danelaw

1545
'Mary Rose' sinks

1628
Duke of Buckingham murdered

1642
St Thomas's severely damaged by Parliamentary cannon fire

1662
Charles II marries Catherine of Braganza in the Governor's house

1665
Sir Bernard de Gomme begins major scheme of fortification

1544
Southsea Castle built

Tudor Period

Stuart Britain

1509
Henry VIII becomes king

1558
Accession of Elizabeth 1

1588
Spanish Armada defeated

1600
Founding of East India Company

1605
Gunpowder Plot

1649
Charles I executed

1666
Great Fire of London

1688-89
Glorious Revolutio

1871
Demolition of fortifications begins

1840
Floating bridge between Portsmouth and Gosport opens

1847
Railway arrives in Portsmouth

1890
New Town Hall opens

1894
Technical Institute established

1910
First slum-clearance scheme

Victorian Britain

Edwardian Era

1837
Victoria becomes queen

1846
Repeal of Corn Laws

1851
Great Exhibition at Crystal Palace

1885
Karl Benz designs first automobile

1899-1902
Boer War

1901
Queen Victoria dies

1903
Campaign for women's suffrage begins

1910
Edward VII dies

HISTORICAL TIMELINE FOR PORTSMOUTH

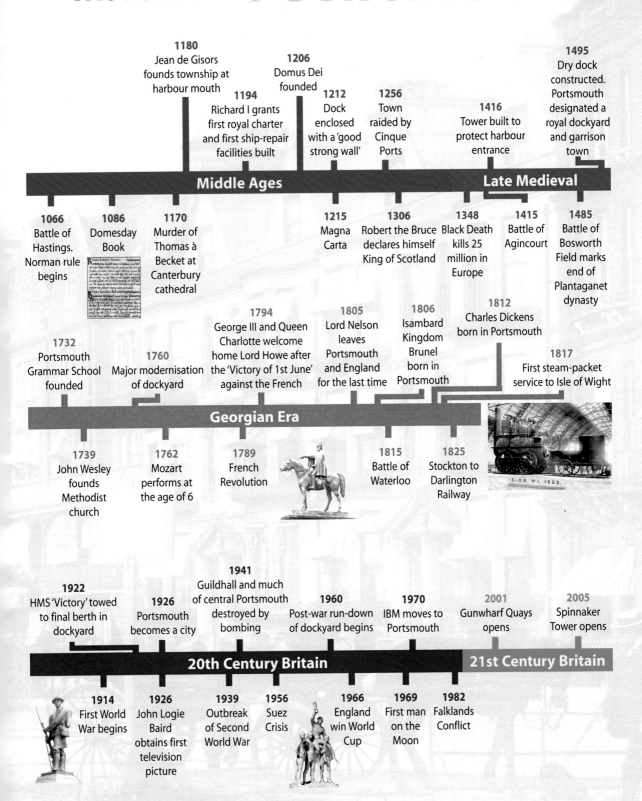

1180 Jean de Gisors founds township at harbour mouth

1206 Domus Dei founded

1194 Richard I grants first royal charter and first ship-repair facilities built

1212 Dock enclosed with a 'good strong wall'

1256 Town raided by Cinque Ports

1416 Tower built to protect harbour entrance

1495 Dry dock constructed. Portsmouth designated a royal dockyard and garrison town

Middle Ages

Late Medieval

1066 Battle of Hastings. Norman rule begins

1086 Domesday Book

1170 Murder of Thomas à Becket at Canterbury cathedral

1215 Magna Carta

1306 Robert the Bruce declares himself King of Scotland

1348 Black Death kills 25 million in Europe

1415 Battle of Agincourt

1485 Battle of Bosworth Field marks end of Plantaganet dynasty

1794 George III and Queen Charlotte welcome home Lord Howe after the 'Victory of 1st June' against the French

1805 Lord Nelson leaves Portsmouth and England for the last time

1806 Isambard Kingdom Brunel born in Portsmouth

1812 Charles Dickens born in Portsmouth

1732 Portsmouth Grammar School founded

1760 Major modernisation of dockyard

1817 First steam-packet service to Isle of Wight

Georgian Era

1739 John Wesley founds Methodist church

1762 Mozart performs at the age of 6

1789 French Revolution

1815 Battle of Waterloo

1825 Stockton to Darlington Railway

1922 HMS 'Victory' towed to final berth in dockyard

1926 Portsmouth becomes a city

1941 Guildhall and much of central Portsmouth destroyed by bombing

1960 Post-war run-down of dockyard begins

1970 IBM moves to Portsmouth

2001 Gunwharf Quays opens

2005 Spinnaker Tower opens

20th Century Britain

21st Century Britain

1914 First World War begins

1926 John Logie Baird obtains first television picture

1939 Outbreak of Second World War

1956 Suez Crisis

1966 England win World Cup

1969 First man on the Moon

1982 Falklands Conflict

CHAPTER ONE

EARLY HISTORY

THE SEA, geography and war, each, between them, have determined the history and development of Portsmouth, and still determine the city's fortunes today. The great natural harbour and, to a lesser extent, neighbouring Langstone Harbour, provide safe anchorages, and the deep water channel which hugs the coast has brought ships safely to these shores over many centuries. Portsmouth's geographical position on the south coast, within easy striking distance of French shores, placed first the area and later, the town itself, firmly on a natural line for sea-borne traffic connecting this country with the continent from the Bronze Age. Finally, and most importantly, Portsmouth has supplied this country with the 'sinews of war' since the late 12th century. A royal dockyard and garrison town since the early Tudor period, Portsmouth flourished when this country was at war and languished in peacetime. It was John Leland, the 16th century traveller and antiquarian, who visited Portsmouth c1540 and noted in his journal that 'the toun of Portesmouth is bare and litle occupied in time of pece'. This is the story of how the sea, geography and war have shaped the history of this city.

The original township was established in the late 12th century, in the southwest corner of a low-lying, marshy island, Portsea Island, which is flanked on the west by Portsmouth Harbour and on the east by Langstone Harbour. Portsea Island's southern shores are lapped by the Solent and sheltered by the Isle of Wight. Its northern shores are separated from the mainland by Portscreek, a narrow channel which links the two harbours. The fertile coastal strip to the north of the creek rises dramatically to the top of Portsdown, the three-hundred-foot-high chalk outlier of the South Downs which runs east to west from the outskirts of Havant to the boundaries of Fareham, and effectively separates Portsmouth from greater Hampshire.

Until fairly recently the low-lying nature of Portsea Island was regarded by historians as something of a deterrent to early settlers. It is no coincidence that the first recorded place name for the Old Portsmouth area - in the Southwick Cartulary - is 'sudewede', Saxon for south wade or water.

However, even if the town as we know it today was not established until the 1180s, increasing amounts of archaeological evidence indicate that there were humans in this area as long ago as the Ice Ages and certainly during the warmer inter-glacial periods. As for the local terrain, far from being a deterrent to settlers, it seems to have facilitated their entry into this part of the country throughout prehistory, that period before written records begin AD 43 with the Roman invasion of the Emperor Claudius. In fact, the whole Solent area lay on an important natural line for sea borne traffic connecting Britain with the continent. The route crossed the Channel between Normandy and Hampshire and grew in importance throughout the Bronze Age and early Iron Age.

It is helpful to consider prehistory generally through its different technological phases: the Stone Age, the Bronze Age and the Iron Age. However; it is necessary to consider the

PORTSMOUTH

Fact File

You will sometimes find the different Stone Age periods described as the Palaeolithic, Mesolithic and Neolithic periods. These are Greek words. Palaeo- means 'early' and -lithic means 'of stone', hence early Stone Age; meso- means 'middle', hence the middle Stone Age, and neo- means 'new', to denote the new group of Stone Age people who came into Britain at this time from mainland Europe.

particular prehistory of what is now a very narrowly defined early 21st century local government area - today's city - within the context of a much more broadly defined geographical area, the greater Portsmouth area, essentially South East Hampshire, an area defined for early man by the sea, by the harbours and inland waterways, by high ground, and by how easily he could move about, feed, shelter and, where necessary, defend himself and his companions.

There is evidence of human activity in this greater Portsmouth area from the early Stone Age when Britain was still physically attached to continental Europe. The evidence exists in the roughly-hewn stone hand axes, some 350,000 years old, found in Solent gravels in the late 19th and early 20th centuries when gravel was still being extracted by hand. Similar hand axes have been found more recently on Portsdown, casual losses, perhaps, of men hunting mammoth and the large herds of bison, horse and reindeer which roamed the land. Flint blades have been found, too, on Long Island and Bakers Island, at the top of Langstone Harbour, which provide more evidence of the activities of early Stone Age peoples exploring - and exploiting - local land and water resources during the Ice Ages.

FARLINGTON MARSHES AT THE TOP OF LANGSTONE HARBOUR 2005 P100701k (Sarah Quail)

LANGSTONE, THE HARBOUR c1955 L481005

LANGSTONE, THE OLD MILL c1955 H481010

LANGSTONE, OLD COTTAGES c1955 L481011

The end of the last glaciation, approximately 8,300 BC, brought significant increases in temperatures and rainfall, and the landscape cover evolved gradually over the next two thousand years into the mixed forests of today. Animal life changed too. The great herds of reindeer, bison and horse, and the mammoth, disappeared with the ice, and smaller forest-loving animals such as boar, aurochs (the now extinct European wild ox), red and roe deer, and elk took their place. Large nomadic hunting parties were no longer necessary and it is probable that smaller social groups existed now to hunt these animals. This was the middle Stone Age.

Evidence suggests that there was a sizeable increase now in population. Almost 500 middle Stone Age sites have been identified in England and Wales compared with little over 100 later early Stone Age sites. There is also evidence on some sites that early man was beginning to supplement his diet of meat with plant foods, fish and shellfish. The upper reaches of both harbours would have provided just such resources for early man in the Portsmouth area and while there is not a lot of evidence of settlement, flints have been identified, washed out by the scour from the brick-earth shores of the islands at the northern end of Langstone Harbour.

LANGSTONE HARBOUR, VELDER LAKE 1856 ZZZ04462 (Portsmouth City Museums and Records Service)

During the New Stone Age, c3,500 BC, a new group of people made their way into Britain, now an island, from northern Europe, bringing with them knowledge of agriculture and domestic animals such as sheep, cattle, pigs and goats. They cleared land with ground or polished stone axes, which gave the era its name. Local flint may well have been used by these immigrants initially, but it is clear from the finds that axes were brought into the area from axe 'factories' as far afield as Wales, Northern Ireland and even Brittany, indicating a significant level of both mobility and long-distance trading links. Flint sickles have been found in the area too, and a stone saddle quern or hand mill was found in Langstone Harbour, which would have been used for grinding cereals to make flour. The new Stone Age farmers also brought pottery manufacture into this country and while no fragments have been identified within the present city boundaries, sherds, or broken pieces of earthenware, have been discovered not far away at Corhampton and near Bedhampton. The building of long earthen mounds - long barrows - in which to bury their dead was a particular feature of new Stone Age society and long barrows, and, later, round barrows, provide the bulk of prehistoric archaeological evidence until the Iron Age and the proliferation of settlement sites. Vestiges remain locally of four long barrows, one in Bedhampton and three in the Meon Valley.

New groups of immigrants entered this country from Northern Europe towards the end of the third millennium BC, bringing with them new funerary traditions characterised by a single inhumation or burial beneath a round barrow, accompanied by a tall pottery vessel called a beaker, which is why the popular description of these people is 'Beaker Folk'. A single example of a beaker burial was excavated in 1926 on Portsdown, reportedly of a young man. Beaker folk also brought with them knowledge of metal-working, but, while we know that metal was in use at the end of the Stone Age, examples of Beaker metal work - purely copper metallurgy - have yet to be discovered in this area, although examples of the succeeding Bronze Age have been discovered locally, as well as burial and settlement sites and hoards.

Burial sites are still the best archaeological sources and several distinct Bronze Age cultural groups have been identified in the area from their different burial traditions. One barrow in the greater Portsmouth area revealed not only an inhumation within a tree-trunk coffin, accompanied by a bi-partite food vessel, but also a cremation accompanied by two bronze daggers. Another 'food vessel' interment has probably been identified at the Southwick Hill crossroads on Portsdown.

Other Bronze Age groups cremated their dead and buried the ashes in urns. An impressive example was excavated at the Southwick Hill crossroads in 1948 when road works necessitated a hurried rescue dig. Amongst the charred bones were the remains of a necklace - sixteen amber beads and 107 disc-shaped shale beads with a gold-covered shale button. They were not burnt and, with the crushed remains of a slotted incense cup, were the grave goods of a richer than average burial. Subsequent road works uncovered the

inhumation of a tall female. Radio carbon dating revealed that she was between fifteen and seventeen years of age when she was buried. Both individuals were probably placed beneath round barrows originally, but ploughing and the wholesale clearance of the area when forts were constructed here in the mid 19th century has stripped Portsdown of what must once have been a rich archaeological site.

Only two significant, mid Bronze Age, settlement sites have been identified locally, both in the greater Portsmouth area, one at Chalton between Portsmouth and Petersfield, and another at West Meon. However, contemporary domestic pottery fragments eroded by the sea from the shores of North Biness Island at the top of Langstone Harbour indicate that there were people living here, but, as yet, no substantial settlement sites have been identified in the immediate vicinity.

However, excavations at Chalton and West Meon do allow us to gain some idea of prehistoric living conditions. The Chalton site, a farmstead, was made up of two circular huts, pits and a possible trackway. Potsherds, a bronze knife and a palstave, a type of bronze axe, were found in the larger of the two huts, and in a pit were found more sherds, a whetstone and a loomweight. There was a hearth in the centre of the smaller hut. The larger hut was probably where the family lived and worked and the smaller one the place where they cooked. The pits were possibly for storage. The site at West Meon was again circular, probably four or five metres in diameter. As at Chalton, there were more pits, and there was evidence that ox, sheep, pigs, horses and birds had frequented the site. Similar settlements must have existed locally, scattered on the higher ground of Portsea Island, along the coastal strip and, as at Chalton, terraced into the chalk slopes of Portsdown.

Of Bronze Age hoards discovered locally, two were found on Portsea Island, on the sites of St Mary's Hospital and St James's Hospital. Palstaves make up the bulk of the material in these hoards but the St James's hoard also contained four armrings, two of which were decorated with an engraved geometric design. Other Bronze Age metalwork found locally includes bronze spearheads and, discovered in Langstone Harbour, a spiral twisted bronze torc, or neckring. The decoration of much of this material suggests that it may have come from Northern France.

Large quantities of bronze and gold were imported into this country from France and Ireland during the Bronze Age, and the recent discovery off Salcombe in Devon of a Bronze Age shipwreck laden with French-made weapons and jewellery, including a solid gold neckring, a gold bracelet, three bronze rapiers, spearheads, axeheads and dagger heads, highlights startlingly the nature and organisation not only of this trade but also of seafaring generally in this period.

Salcombe's own impressive natural harbour may well have been a far more important trading centre than has been previously thought. The sort of boat which foundered off Salcombe could equally have navigated local coastal waters. It was probably some

dozen metres long, about two metres wide and constructed of oak planks lashed together with yew withies, made watertight with mosses and beeswax. In the light of this discovery and the casual finds made locally, it may be timely to reassess the relative importance of both Portsmouth and Langstone harbours as Bronze Age trading centres.

Burial sites cease to provide the bulk of archaeological evidence in the succeeding Iron Age. The increasing number of settlement sites identified and excavated are now the major sources of information. Some dozen Iron Age sites have been excavated in the Portsmouth area. Within the present city boundaries, an Iron Age site was discovered on the Portsdown George Inn site ahead of roadworks at the junction of the A3 and B2177. It was made of living, working and storage areas. Another Iron Age site has been identified at the Southwick Hill crossroads, again in advance of roadworks.

Iron Age salt production sites have also been observed locally with particular concentrations at the tops of both Portsmouth and Langstone harbours. The site on the Paulsgrove foreshore at the top of Portsmouth Harbour was excavated because erosion by the sea was threatening to destroy the site. Briquetage remains were identified, pieces of the clay vessels and moulds used in the salt-extraction process.

Hill forts and defensive works are features now of the local landscape, reflecting, perhaps, developing social structures. Old Winchester Hill above the Meon Valley is the best local example and may well have been

BUTSER ANCIENT FARM

Four miles south of Petersfield, just off the A3, is the Butser Ancient Farm, a replica of the sort of farm which existed during the Iron Age, c300 BC. There are buildings, structures and occasionally animals, fields and crops which existed at this time. However, it is not only a museum. It prides itself also on being a large open-air laboratory where research is undertaken into the Iron Age and the succeeding Roman period. The design of the replica farm is based soundly on evidence from original sites: ditches, banks, postholes, pits, pottery, pollen and carbonized material. It is the only place in Western Europe where all the varieties of prehistoric wheat can be seen growing in fields. Special open days are held regularly for both school groups and the general public, when 'living history' teams of actors show just what it was like to be an inhabitant of Iron Age Britain.

PETERSFIELD, BUTSER ANCIENT FARM 2005 P48721k (Sarah Quail)

an important local centre having a wide area of influence. Another possible defensive enclave in the area may exist on Hayling Island. Tournerbury is a single wall ringwork where Iron Age sherds have been found. Surprisingly, no defensive works have been discovered on Portsdown, but more modest earthworks have been identified - lynchet and enclosure banks, and ditches, evidence of prehistoric ploughing and cultivation terraces, as well as boundaries.

An extremely rare late Iron Age shrine constructed possibly in the mid 1st century AD has also been discovered locally, again on Hayling Island. It is overlaid by the later Romano-Celtic temple. The Iron Age shrine consisted of a circular building or enclosure surrounded by a quadrangular enclosure. A wealth of material has been found on the site - clasps, buckles, brooches, bracelets, finger rings, beads, harness, bridle bits, military equipment and coins, local issues as well as coinage from Gaul, the Roman province of Western Europe, and Armorica (the future Brittany), much of it votive offerings, gifts dedicated to the god or gods who were worshipped there.

Coinage first appeared in Britain c150 BC from northern Europe, and four of the five earliest known examples of British copies of these early coins have been found within a ten-mile radius of Portsmouth, two of them on the slopes of Portsdown, above Portchester. They were probably made, and used, by a local tribal group, from roughly 80 BC. No examples have been found locally of the first British coins to bear an inscription - those of

Commius, who was sent to Britain by Julius Caesar in 55 BC to persuade the Britons to submit to Roman rule. However, coins have been found locally bearing the names of his sons. One was found near Fareham and others were found at the Hayling Island Iron Age shrine. A late Iron Age hoard was actually discovered in Portsmouth in 1830. While the hoard itself does not appear to have survived, there are, in the British Museum, nine coins which came from Portsmouth in 1830 and are most likely from this hoard. They include coins from several of the different tribal states of this period. There is a silver coin from the Durotiges, whose stronghold was the great fortress of Maiden Castle in Dorset, two coins of the Iceni of East Anglia and several from areas in northern France.

Prehistory finishes with the appearance of names on coins. In AD 43, the Roman expeditionary force led by Plautius landed at Richborough behind the Isle of Thanet. Britain was absorbed now into the Roman Empire and its history incorporated into, and recounted in, the texts of the ancient writers. However, our knowledge of Roman Britain is still very heavily dependent on archaeological evidence.

Surviving Romano-British pottery in this area spans all four centuries of Roman rule AD 43-c410 and is vital to our understanding of Roman settlement around Portsmouth. It is low-status material, though, used for everyday food preparation, serving and storage purposes, and although the villa system was growing steadily along the Hampshire coast by the end of the 1st century AD, there is no evidence from either quantity or quality of pottery recovered locally to suggest that there was any large-scale or high-status settlement in the area, despite the fact that both Portsmouth and Langstone harbours were ideally placed for both coastal and cross-Channel trade, and the present A27 must have become a significant east-west route from the mid 1st century AD. This is all the more curious, given the fact that only a few miles to the west was a Roman supply base at Fishbourne, established very early in the Roman military occupation, AD 43, which, in due course, developed into the magnificent Roman palace and important provincial centre of the local client king, Cogidubnus.

However, Fishbourne lay in the territory of the Atrebates, a tribe with a long history of allegiance to Rome. There were certainly tribes hostile to the Roman invaders on the Isle of Wight and their proximity may

have deterred the Romans from pushing any further westward initially. The sea levels also appear to have been rising during the 2nd and 3rd centuries AD, which may have made lower-lying coastal sites unattractive to later settlers and have driven those people already there further inland.

By the late 3rd century, though, there was some significant development locally. Military surveyors were examining the local coast for possible sites for a fortress. North Sea pirates had broken through the Dover straits and were engaged in launching damaging raids on the Roman provinces on both sides of the Channel. The Belgian sailor Carausius was charged to rid these shores of the insurgents. The great walled fortress built by Carausius at the top of Portsmouth Harbour was part of a defensive line of similar forts - the forts of the 'Saxon Shore' - stretching from the Wash to the Solent.

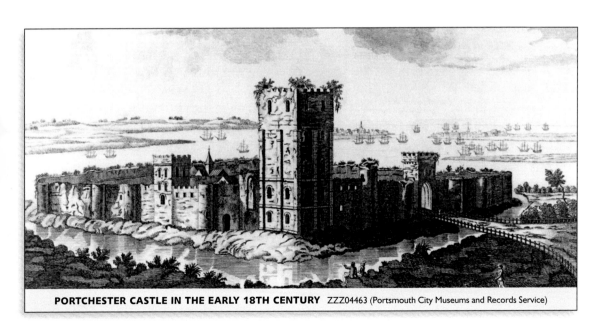

PORTCHESTER CASTLE IN THE EARLY 18TH CENTURY ZZZ04463 (Portsmouth City Museums and Records Service)

PORTCHESTER CASTLE 2005 P100703k (Sarah Quail)

This view was taken from Port Solent.

Portchester is a formidable piece of military engineering even today. Its massive walls are ten feet thick and were originally over 20 feet high. They enclose an area of nine acres. A series of hollow D-shaped bastions project from the curtain walls. They were probably all floored originally at parapet level to support an artillery piece, most likely a ballista. Such forward platforms were a relatively new phenomenon and, in this fortress, built to defend anchorage and hinterland, we have the first of the remarkable series of defensive positions built in the Portsmouth area over the next almost two thousand years.

Military occupation of the site ceased cAD 370, but there is evidence that in the last years of the Roman era, the site was occupied by, and gave some protection to, a small civilian population who may well have cultivated the area inside the fort. These were very uncertain times. The Picts and the Scots were attacking Britain from the north and the Saxons were attacking in the south. By the early 5th century, Rome had virtually cut all links with Britain and left the country to fend for itself.

There is strong evidence to suggest that the Isle of Wight and the Hampshire coast were settled originally by Jutes - Germanic people from Jutland - who settled first in Kent and then moved westwards, bypassing the Saxons from the north-German coastlands who had settled in Sussex. In due course, this Jutish outlier was itself overrun by the West Saxons. The West Saxon Annals in the 'Anglo-Saxon Chronicle' record that in 501, 'Port came to Britain with his two sons Bieda and Maegla and two ships at the place called Portes mutha and slew a young Britain, a very noble man'. Whatever the exact truth of this record based on 9th-century recollections of a late 5th- or early 6th-century memory of a landing in the Portsmouth area, the event is believed to have taken place at or near Portchester and it is not impossible that resistance came from a local leader using the fortress as his base.

As for 'Portes mutha' itself, it is certainly not the area we know today as Old Portsmouth. It is most likely the river mouth or estuary of the River Wallington, in the north west corner of the harbour, near the fort at Portchester. It is, however, the first time the place name 'Portsmouth' is recorded in a written source.

The new invaders, in their turn, seem to have settled quickly into the Portchester area. Excavations - typical Saxon pottery of the period - have yielded evidence of

PORTCHESTER CASTLE, THE WATER GATE AND WALLS 2005 ZZZ04464 (Author's Collection)

THE FIRST ENGLISH NAVAL BATTLE

The first English naval battle is believed to have taken place at the top of Portsmouth Harbour in AD 896. The events are described in 'The Anglo-Saxon Chronicle'. Apparently, King Alfred's ships intercepted six Viking raiders in an unidentified river mouth or harbour on the South Coast. Exmouth, Poole Harbour, the Hamble and Spithead all fit the description. The battle site consisted of three areas: an outer bay, a river mouth or harbour entrance and an upper harbour.

The Vikings had beached three of their ships, possibly to find water. They were covered by the remaining ships offshore. The English set on these ships, capturing two and killing all hands. The third got away. Three English ships now grounded on the same side of the harbour as the Vikings and, as the tide ebbed further, fighting broke out between the two sides on the exposed land. The rising tide put an end to the battle and the lighter Viking ships got away, but their oarsmen were exhausted and many were wounded. Only one ship got clean away. The remaining two surrendered, probably off the Owers Bank at Selsey.

Did the original battle take place at the top of Portsmouth Harbour? Military historian Richard Brooks is sure that it did. Local yachtsmen tell him that the tideflow described by the chroniclers is very similar to that at the mouth of Fareham Creek, off Portchester, a settlement of some significance and therefore a possible Viking target. He also feels that if the battle had taken place further west, the Viking oarsmen would hardly have made it beyond the Portland race and the waters round the Isle of Wight. They would certainly not have made it as far as Selsey. It should also be noted that the Domesday Survey records that Edward the Confessor reduced Fareham's tax liability because it was exposed to Viking incursions.

intensive occupation of the fort itself from the late 5th or early 6th century. There is also evidence of substantial 8th- and 9th-century structures.

The fort acquired a new defensive role in the early 10th century, when Viking raids were threatening Britain's south coast. A number of former fortified enclaves, many with Roman walls, were repaired and designated as defended settlements, or burhs, protected by a semi-civilian militia. Portchester was one of these designated settlements and is listed as such in the early 10th century document known as the 'Burghal Hidage'.

For lack of any significant archaeological evidence, we know very little about human activity on Portsea Island itself at this time. Rising sea levels may have deterred settlers, although the recent discovery of the remains of a small 6th-century boat at the top of Langstone Harbour points to some level of activity. A few fragments of late Saxon pottery were found in excavations at Kingston

'THE DOMESDAY BOOK'

'The Domesday Book' is one of the most famous documents of English history. It is a survey of England commissioned by William the Conqueror 20 years after his conquest of England. He wanted to know how much each manor was worth in the time of his predecessor, what it was worth at the time of the Conquest, and what it was worth now in 1085-6.

The survey is an extraordinary record of life in late 11th-century England. For each manor listed, there are personal names, the number of ploughs, lists of freemen, villagers and slaves, the amount of woodland, pasture and meadow, lists of mills, fish ponds and salt pans and how many different animals there were, as well as information on what the manor was worth.

The king's officials visited over 3,000 different places in the course of only one year and the final document was assembled at Winchester by a monk. It is kept today in the National Archives at Kew.

Crescent in the 1970s, but the spread of buildings across Portsea Island in the course of the 19th and 20th centuries has probably destroyed what evidence there may have been of early settlement.

The 'Domesday Survey' of 1086 lists some three pre-Conquest, ie Saxon, manors on Portsea Island: Buckland, Copnor and Fratton, each lying towards the centre of the island on what little high ground exists, but they are of little value compared to their mainland neighbours. There is no reference to any church building on Portsea Island before 1164 - a church would have been a sure sign of an established community nearby - but recent investigations at St Mary's Portsea show that there may be a structure beneath the footprint of the current church building predating what has been understood until now to be the original,

12th-century structure. Further work is planned to try and substantiate the claim. If there was an earlier church building here or, possibly, a pagan shrine, it raises important questions about the relative status of pre-Conquest settlement on Portsea Island.

Fact File

Why is 'The Domesday Book' so-called?

'The Domesday Book' is so-called because it brought doom and gloom to the population. As there was such a detailed record now of their assets, people could no longer argue about their tax liabilities! The decision was final - as it will be on Judgement Day, or Domesday, when your soul is judged!

THE ENTRANCE TO FAREHAM CREEK 2005 P100704k (Sarah Quail)

Further work is also required to tease out the confused relationship between Portchester and its environs and Portes mutha. The place-name 'Portes mutha' is certainly associated with the upper reaches of Portsmouth Harbour before the late 12th century and there is circumstantial evidence that a community of some importance had developed there. Portchester's military potential seems to have been acknowledged at an early stage by the Normans, who needed not only to consolidate their hold on the country after 1066 but also to maintain good lines of communication with their possessions in Northern and Western France, and early in the 12th century the fortress was acquired by the Crown.

There are indiscriminate references to Portsmouth in official records of the early years of the 12th century as a point of departure and return for king and court to and from Normandy. This is certainly not the community at the harbour mouth, and although serious work on the new castle within the fortress walls was not underway until later in the century, there is archaeological evidence of a large, late-Saxon building, possibly a great hall, which would have provided appropriate royal lodgings, before the new accommodation had been completed. Outside the castle walls, it looks as if Portchester may have been a royal borough, although no charter of incorporation has ever been identified. More importantly, the 'Domesday Survey' records that Fareham had by far the highest population of any local community. Significantly, it is noted there that Edward the Confessor reduced Fareham's tax liability 'because being on the coast, it was exposed to the incursions of northern pirates'. In short, it was a prize worth the Vikings' taking.

Whatever the status of this community at the top of the harbour, by the end of the 12th century, the place name 'Portes mutha', or Portsmouth, was now firmly and irrevocably associated with a new township, one planted deliberately in the south-west corner of Portsea Island at the harbour mouth.

FAREHAM, CAMS MILL ZZZ04465 (From Gates)

FAREHAM, CAMS MILL ZZZ04466 (From Gates)

Two views of Cams Mill, Fareham, reputedly the oldest tidal mill in England. These are taken from Fareham Creek and the road above.

CHAPTER TWO

THE 'VILL OF PORTSMOUTH'

THE NEW township at the harbour mouth was founded by a wealthy French merchant and landowner called Jean de Gisors c1180. He had interests in the Portsmouth area already.

A STAINED GLASS WINDOW IN PORTSMOUTH CATHEDRAL ZZZ04488 (Author's Collection)

This window portrays Jean de Gisors.

His grandfather, Thibaud de Gisors, had been granted the manor of Titchfield by William the Conqueror's son and successor as king, William Rufus, for services which he, Thibaud, had rendered the English side in Normandy in the struggles between the English and the French in the early 12th century.

Jean de Gisors was probably drawn to the site at the harbour mouth by its potential for developing cross-channel trading links. The community at the top of the harbour was ceasing to be an attractive option for development as the northern reaches were now silting up significantly.

Many new towns were established in the 12th and 13th centuries, including at least eleven in Hampshire. The 'new' Portsmouth conforms very much to the general pattern. It was built on the initiative of the lord of the manor on a well-established grid pattern of streets and lanes. A marketplace was designated and settlers encouraged to move into the town on favourable terms in the hope of long-term financial benefit accruing to the lord of the manor and his family from developing trade. In fact, it is more than likely that Portsmouth's fair and market, which were granted formally in the first Royal Charter of 1194, had been established some years before by Jean de Gisors.

There were other advantages to this new site. The harbour, of course, provided a safe anchorage, but a settlement just inside the harbour mouth and near the deep-water channel and open sea could take larger ships than the site at the top of the harbour. The shingle spit at the harbour entrance also provided additional protection for ships within its lee. The Camber, as it has been called from that day to this, provided an obvious site for a quayside - the Town Quay, as it became subsequently known.

Portchester Castle also provided some protection for the new township. By the end of the 12th century, the Norman castle in the Inner Bailey was complete. It was used regularly by Henry II on his journeys between England and Normandy. It was at Portchester, in 1164, that Henry received the Bishop of Evreux on his mission to mediate between the king and Becket. The king was at Portchester again in 1172 on his way to France to plead, before papal legates, his innocence of any complicity in Becket's death. Important prisoners were confined at Portchester and treasure was sent regularly from Winchester to Portchester for shipment to Normandy.

THE LANDS OF THE KINGS OF ENGLAND IN WESTERN FRANCE ZZZ04489 (Caen City Council)

Jean de Gisors himself was also well acquainted with the Plantagenets. His own father had served Henry I faithfully until the latter's death in 1135, and the castle at Gisors, an important town on the border between the Duchy of Normandy and the French kingdom, was a regular meeting place between the kings of France and England throughout the 1170s and 1180s. Jean de Gisors was, in fact, civil governor of Gisors until Henry II put himself in possession of the town c1164.

The first references to Jean de Gisors and Portsmouth occur in the Southwick Cartularies. Between 1164 and 1177, Jean de Gisors purchased the manor of Buckland

THE GRANT OF THE SITE FOR A CHAPEL DEDICATED TO ST THOMAS OF CANTERBURY
ZZZ04490 (Hampshire Record Office)

This shows an extract from the Southwick Cartulary.

WARBLINGTON, THE CHURCH OF ST THOMAS OF CANTERBURY c1955 W648017

WARBLINGTON CASTLE AND MANOR HOUSE, THE REMAINS c1955 W648016

from the de Port family. It covered the south-western part of the island, including the area we know today as Old Portsmouth, where the new settlement was established. A subsequent reference occurs in a gift Jean de Gisors made c1180-6 to Southwick Priory of a site for the erection of a chapel 'in honour of the glorious martyr, Thomas of Canterbury, formerly Archbishop', on 'his land called sudewede on the island of Portsea'.

The dedication is interesting. A great cult devoted to Becket developed rapidly across Western Europe soon after his death, and many new churches were dedicated to his memory, including nearby Warblington

parish church. The de Gisors family had particular cause to remember him, for, in the 1160s, the exiled Archbishop of Canterbury spent some time in Gisors and a chapel within the castle precincts was dedicated to him shortly after his death. As the first family, the de Gisors family must have met Becket, and the dedication of the chapel in the new settlement of Portsmouth must reflect this earlier connection. Interestingly, several centuries later, Warblington Castle was the home of Margaret de la Pole, the last of the Plantagenets and the mother of Cardinal Reginald Pole, who was executed by Henry VIII.

Fact File
Southwick Priory

Southwick Priory was a monastery that followed the rule of St Augustine. It was established by Henry I in the 1120s within the walls of Portchester Castle. The priory church, built c1130, still stands. Within 20 years, the canons moved to a less cramped site on the other side of Portsdown Hill, in the village of Southwick where they stayed until 1538. Documents relating to land and buildings given to the priory can be seen in the Hampshire Record Office in Winchester.

Southwick Priory was dissolved in 1538 and the site granted to John White, whose descendants still own it. Southwick House was requisitioned in 1944 by the Allied Expeditionary Force and Eisenhower launched the D-Day offensive from there.

SOUTHWICK PRIORY ZZZ04491 (Portsmouth Cathedral)

Another gift to Southwick, made between 1185 and 1194, was a messuage, a dwelling house with outbuildings and land, no longer on his land called 'sudewede' but 'in my vill of Portsmouth', the rents to be put towards keeping the new chapel in good repair.

These gifts from Jean de Gisors to the canons of Southwick, as well as later ones, chronicle the early history of the new community.

Among other things, there are references to individuals, to Portsmouth's first residents. There are also references to the first street names, such as New North Street, perhaps today's High Street. There is also a description of a watermill. Sometime between 1189 and 1194, Jean de Gisors gave a tithe, ie a tenth of the annual revenue of his watermill 'on the arm of the sea north of the vill of Portsmouth' to Southwick Priory. This is the mill known subsequently as the King's Mill, which was situated roughly where the main entrance to the Gunwharf stood, later HMS 'Vernon', and

REFERENCE TO THE NEW TOWN AT THE HARBOUR MOUTH ZZZ04492 (Hampshire Records Office)

This photograph from the Southwick Cartularies is the first known reference to the 'new town at the harbour mouth'.

where, today, visitors enter Gunwharf Quays.

The new town was a classic example of a deliberately planned early medieval town like Salisbury or Ludlow. Streets, houses for the new residents, the site of the chapel and the marketplace, were all laid out by Jean de Gisors' agent or steward, just as today's builders lay out a new housing development. However, Jean de Gisors and his family did not benefit long from the revenues coming in from his new development. He forfeited all his English property, including Portsmouth, to the Crown in 1194 - for backing the king's brother, Prince John, when the king, Richard I, was a prisoner of the German Emperor, Henry VI.

It is not difficult to see why Jean de Gisors backed Prince John. On his way home overland from the ill-fated 3rd Crusade, the king had fallen into the hands of Duke Leopold of Austria and his overlord, the German Emperor, shortly before Christmas 1192. The French king, Philippe Auguste, seized this auspicious moment to over-run Normandy, the English royal family's ancestral heartland in France, and was threatening to invade

---

Fact File

Portsmouth Cathedral

Portsmouth Cathedral is the oldest surviving building in Portsmouth. The original chancel and transepts are part of the chapel built on the instructions of Jean de Gisors in the 1180s. They are impressive in scale. Money was clearly not stinted on the project. Nikolaus Pevsner, in the 'Hampshire' volume of 'The Buildings of England' series, describes St Thomas's as having 'more of the character of a miniature cathedral or monastic church'.

33

England, while in England itself, Prince John, hoping to supplant Richard, rebelled.

With financial interests on both sides of the Channel, Jean de Gisors, and many other men like him, had to decide which way to jump. Unfortunately for him, he backed the wrong side. The king's mother, the redoubtable and resourceful dowager, Queen Eleanor, widow of Henry II, rallied those nobles loyal to the king, exacted oaths of allegiance, rapidly put what physical defences there were into better order and reinforced their garrisons. There was a general muster and so efficient was the watch kept on the east coast that the French fleet did not dare land. Prince John and his supporters were besieged in their strongholds, and ransom terms successfully negotiated for the king's release.

The king landed at Sandwich on 13 March 1194. John's rebellion collapsed, his partisans and known supporters fled - and their lands were confiscated. Exchequer records note that 'Portsmouth is an escheat of the lord king and is worth with its belongings £20' and 'Titchfield is an escheat of the lord king as it was land of the Normans'.

Land which was confiscated by the Crown was usually sold on promptly to whoever was prepared to pay the best price. The king's financial needs were pressing. He had still to pay the balance owing on his ransom and he had to find the resources to assemble a fleet and put an army into the field to wrest back Normandy from the French king. Much of the land of John's supporters was therefore sold on, but the king did not dispose of Portsmouth. As stated in the city's first royal charter, granted by the king to local residents on 2 May 1194, the king 'retained' the town in his own hands. The reasons were simple - sea, geography and war.

Richard I, like Jean de Gisors before him, could see the strategic importance of this township beside the sea. It lay on an administrative axis stretching from the old Norman ducal capital of Rouen to Caen, a town which had been growing in importance during the 12th century and where Richard's father, Henry II, had established the Norman Exchequer in 1172 in the great fortress built by William the Conqueror. From Caen, it was an easy journey across the Channel to Portsmouth and from there to the old Saxon capital of Winchester, where the English treasury was still located. Portsmouth would be a useful link in this chain of communication. Unlike in Southampton, there was no powerful merchant class in Portsmouth likely to frustrate the king and his designs. During Richard's reign, many loads of treasure were shipped across the Channel through Portsmouth. The harbour was also a useful rendezvous and haven for ships transporting troops, and had plenty of space ashore to assemble men and supplies for military campaigns. The town prospered in the remaining years of Richard's reign.

He put the town's facilities to good use immediately. Men and ships were summoned to Portsmouth, where he joined them on 25 April, anxious to put to sea at once. The weather was not promising, though. When he tried to sail on 2 May, in the teeth of a gale, he was forced to put back into port. The

AN 18TH-CENTURY INK SKETCH OF THE CHATEAU OF CAEN ZZZ04494 (Caen City Council)

weather did not improve sufficiently for him to attempt the crossing again for another ten days. It was during his brief stay in the town at this time that Richard granted Portsmouth its first royal charter. Portsmouth was now a royal borough, independent of county administration. The town was entitled to hold a fair annually for fifteen days and a weekly market. It was also granted exemption from a wide range of different tolls and exactions, and given criminal jurisdiction within its boundaries.

All sides could be pleased with the deal. Portsmouth now joined the ranks of those other towns in England, many much larger, such as Norwich, Ipswich, Lincoln and Gloucester, who also acquired similar

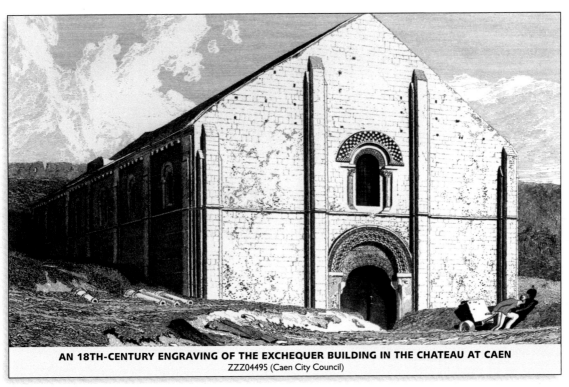

AN 18TH-CENTURY ENGRAVING OF THE EXCHEQUER BUILDING IN THE CHATEAU AT CAEN
ZZZ04495 (Caen City Council)

privileges at this time. The king brought firmly under royal control an important new strategic position on the south coast. There was no risk now of a powerful merchant group emerging which might threaten the military and naval role planned for Portsmouth. Work began immediately on the construction of appropriate accommodation for king and court. Described variously as the King's House or the king's houses, the new buildings occupied a site at the top of Penny Street belonging today to Portsmouth Grammar School, but known as Kingshall Green for much of its history. In due course, a great hall with cellars, a chapel and domestic buildings was constructed on the site, surrounded by walls and a ditch.

Records show that large sums of money were spent at this time on the king's houses, their defence and other works in the town, including, possibly, ship repair facilities. A separate set of accounts had to be established in the Exchequer to record expenditure. They itemise not only the large sums of money passing through the town for transport to Normandy, and the costs of the building works, but also such domestic expenditure as the 14 tonnels of wine unloaded and placed in the cellars of the King's House and what it cost to take the king's hawks to Normandy with 'engines of war'. These were probably wooden structures capable of hurling missiles at the enemy, or even wooden towers on wheels for siege work. The accounts also record the considerable numbers of fighting men moved through Portsmouth at this time in ships requisitioned specifically for such purposes.

As for the ship repair facilities, these may well have been part and parcel of the king's plans for making Portsmouth the base for his galleys on the English side of the Channel. At the same time as work began in Portsmouth, similar developments were taking place on the Seine, at Les Andelys, midway between Le Havre and Paris, beneath Richard's great castle of Chateau Gaillard. Les Andelys would be the base for the galleys in Normandy. Richard's successor, his brother, John, is usually the one credited with establishing Portsmouth dockyard in the early 13th century, but it is looking increasingly likely that Richard should have the credit for this initiative some 30 years previously.

Little survives above ground today of the late 12th-century town other than the medieval grid pattern of streets and the chancel and transepts of St Thomas's Church, now Portsmouth Cathedral. Excavations undertaken between 1968 and 1971 in Oyster Street - on the site of the medieval quayside - did uncover something of the original settlement, however. There was evidence of permanent occupation from the late 12th century, clearly identified from a combination of stratigraphy and structural remains - beam slots or gulleys, post holes, hearths and depressions - and ceramic and other finds. There is evidence of at least two permanent buildings in the earliest occupation levels, and a complex of buildings, a well and water cistern in the 13th- and 14th- century levels when the town was beginning to grow in size.

PORTSMOUTH'S SEALS

The earliest example of the use of the common seal survives on a deed which was executed between 1245 and 1260. Then, as now, the device is a ship with castle, a small wooden tower on the deck, used when engaged in a sea battle, and a furled sail with a crescent on the left of the mast and a star on the right. The official seal of the bailiff is first mentioned in a deed of 1282. This device - a star over a crescent moon - is identical with the seal of William of Longchamp, bishop of Ely and Richard I's chancellor, which was used to seal Portsmouth's first charter in May 1194, the Great Seal having been lost during the king's travels.

The bishop accompanied Richard to the Holy Land in 1190-94 and it is not too fanciful to speculate that he adopted the star over the crescent moon - Muslim devices - for his own seal during this period. It is also tempting to suggest that Portsmouth's first bailiffs simply copied the seal on their first royal charter - Longchamp's seal - for their own purposes. It is still used today by the Lord Mayor. The same common seal is also still in use today to authenticate Portsmouth City Council documents.

A system of local government was in place by the early 13th century. There are references to town officials and a borough court in both the Southwick Cartularies and in Exchequer records. References to a common seal occur from the 1240s and by the end of the century there is definitely a mayor and a common seal in use to authenticate official documents.

The city's medieval records do not survive. They are believed to have been destroyed during one or other of the devastating French raids on the town in the later medieval period, but a 16th-century 'Customs and Usages of Portsmouth' survives, which, from internal evidence - names of individuals - must have been drafted in the late 13th century and may well contain even earlier material. It sheds interesting light on town life in the early medieval period.

Portsmouth in the Past
BY
WILLIAM G. GATES.
· · · · · ·

Topographical Notes and Sketches
reprinted from the
"Hampshire Telegraph." 1925

—
PORTSMOUTH:
CHARPENTIER Ltd., 46, HIGH STREET.
1926.
THE DEVICE ON THE MAYOR'S SEAL
ZZZ04533 (From Gates)

THE 'CUSTOMS AND USAGES'

It is clear from this document that by the late 13th century, at least, the town was governed by a mayor and bailiff; there were two constables, two clerk-serjeants, twelve jurors and 'the comoyns'. The jurors were those men elected, probably by a show of hands of 'the comoyns' at a public meeting, perhaps in the church or churchyard, to help the mayor and bailiff govern the town. The constables and clerk-serjeants were employed to carry out their orders.

Arrangements are noted here for the smooth transfer, each year, of power from one mayor and his officers to the next, with the common seal, the town's records - 'the chartures with all the evidences that longith to the Town' - and the weights and measures. There are rules and regulations for dealing with trading issues, the management of the town fields, and livestock within the town, how cases will be brought and heard in the borough court, how the market is to be regulated and rights of common - a cartful of wood and a deer - in neighbouring forests. There is also detail on the payment of taxes and the gruesome punishment meted out to wrong-doers. Thieves convicted of taking goods up to the value of 12d would be nailed to the pillory by the ear. If you sold underweight goods, you could be put in the pillory. Scolds were tipped into the Camber in the ducking-stool and thieves were branded and their eyes put out. If one man slew another, he was burnt to death at Cattecleffe, an area on the present naval base. A woman who killed a man was tied to a stake at Cattecleffe at low water and left there for the rising tide to 'ov'flowe her'.

Richard I died prematurely in Aquitaine in 1199 of a gangrenous wound. He was succeeded by his brother, Prince John. John was not a successful soldier. Within five years, he had lost Normandy to the French. The loss of Normandy in 1204 was regarded initially as only a temporary setback. A fleet of unprecedented size was mobilised at Portsmouth at Whitsun 1205 to convey an army across the Channel to recover Normandy. In the event, this particular fleet never put to sea, but it was the first of the many expeditionary forces summoned to Portsmouth in this and succeeding centuries.

During the 13th and 14th centuries, the town was a rendezvous for expeditions, not only to Normandy, but to Poitou and, particularly, Gascony. Ships were dispatched to Portsmouth from most of the English ports to convey men, horses, other supplies and weapons across the Channel. If the number of conveyances of houses in the town is any measure, the town would seem to have been of a fair size by the early 13th century. Some of the houses even had upper rooms, or solars. Money was still being spent on the town, too. John had the dock at Portsmouth enclosed with a good, strong wall for the better protection of his ships and galleys and he had stores built for tackle and other equipment. He also enlarged and improved accommodation at the King's House. In 1254, the Great Council of the Realm itself met in Portsmouth.

Besides its role as a rendezvous for expeditionary forces, Portsmouth also began to develop now as a trading centre. A considerable trade developed with northern and western Europe. Wheat, in particular, was exported to France and Spain, in addition to the wheat sent out from Portsmouth to the troops in the field during the French wars. Wool was also exported. The chief import was wine from Bayonne and Bordeaux. Other goods from France included woad, wax and iron. Henry III granted the town a gild merchant in 1256. This was an important landmark in the development of the town, but shortly afterwards the momentum for development began to falter. It was becoming increasingly obvious that Normandy was unlikely to be recovered. The town was raided in 1265 by the barons of the Cinque Ports, envious, perhaps, of this new trading rival, and they left a trail of destruction in their wake. By the end of the century, there were reports that both the King's House and Portchester Castle were in dire need of repair, sure signs that official use for and, therefore, interest in the town had ceased. By 1336, the town could muster only two vessels, one out of repair, to answer the king's summons to send him all their vessels above a certain size.

It suffered grievously during the Hundred Years War. Early in 1338, the first of four French raids on the town took place when ships and galleys from Normandy landed, plundered and burnt the town. Only the parish church and Domus Dei, the hospice founded by Peter des Roches, bishop of Winchester, in the early 13th century escaped serious damage, being built of stone. While many of the dwelling houses may have had stone footings and even stone cellars, they were constructed for the most part of wood. Similar raids in 1369, 1377 and 1380 ruined Portsmouth and its trade. The inhabitants were so impoverished in both 1338 and 1369 that they were released from paying taxes. The town's fortunes were at a low ebb by the early 1380s.

A reassessment of its strategic importance - as a port of embarkation - did not come soon enough. Clearly the issue of the town's defences needed to be addressed, and in 1386 a commission was appointed to survey the town and take appropriate action. A simple earthwork was probably put up now round the town, and later, between 1416 and 1420, a tower was erected to guard the harbour entrance on the site of the present Round Tower, which dates from the Tudor period.

A major incident took place in Portsmouth in 1450 when Adam Moleyns, bishop of Chichester, was murdered within the precincts of the Domus Dei. It was said at the time that he was set upon by soldiers and sailors, aggrieved that they had not been paid their wages, but it was more likely a political assassination, procured by enemies of the king, Henry VI, and his hated advisers. Whatever the real truth of the matter, the

Church held Portsmouth and its people responsible for the crime and they were all excommunicated. They were absolved of the crime only in 1508. For almost 60 years there were, in theory, no services or religious ceremonies of any sort, no burials and no ringing of bells. When the ban was lifted, it was claimed that this had been a period of unparalleled hardship for the town, but the evidence does not altogether substantiate this claim.

The wool and wine trades still carried on, but it was only in the early Tudor period that the town's economic life revived significantly. Henry VII was sufficiently alarmed by growing French activity in the Channel to commission the building of the Square Tower in 1494, and the construction of a bulwark, a defensive earthwork, to protect the town on the seaward side. The following year, he ordered a dry dock to be built on a site a little to the north of the town, near to the present site of HMS 'Victory'. There had been docking, i.e. ship repair facilities, in the vicinity since John's reign certainly and, probably, even Richard's. There is also evidence that there were already related buildings alongside the site of this new facility - the offices of the clerk of the king's ships, a storehouse and a forge - before building work began, but it was the construction of this new dock between 1495 and 1496 which not only revived the town's flagging economy, but launched what would become by the 18th century the great industrial enterprise of Portsmouth Dockyard.

DOMUS DEI

If there is a hot summer, you can make out, on the grass of Governor's Green, the footings of the buildings which made up the complex of the Domus Dei (God's House), or the Governor's House, as it became in the late 16th century. It was one of a number of similar hospices or hospitals established in coastal towns or near the sea, not only to receive pilgrims and strangers on their way to a famous shrine, but also to care for local people, if need be. Portsmouth was well-placed for the great pre-Reformation shrines of Winchester and Chichester, as well as for the medieval shrines of northern Europe.

This hospice was dedicated to St Nicholas. It consisted of a long hall divided into bays by pillars. At one end, was a porch and at the other, a chapel. The central part of the hall was left free and occupants slept, or were nursed, in the aisles. The government was vested in a master. Brethren, assisted by sisters, nursed and cooked. The spiritual care of the residents and travellers was entrusted to priest chaplains.

After the complex was dissolved in 1538 by Henry VIII and the brethren had dispersed, the buildings seem to have been abandoned until the late 16th century, when Portsmouth's governor quit the rather sparse accommodation of the Square Tower and moved in. His successors stayed there until the 19th century. In due course, the site was cleared of all the ancillary buildings, leaving only the early 13th century chapel, now the garrison church. The church was partially destroyed by wartime bombing, but has been left standing, its nave open to the skies, as a permanent war memorial.

THE GARRISON CHURCH c1900 ZZZ04493 (Portsmouth City Museums and Records Service)

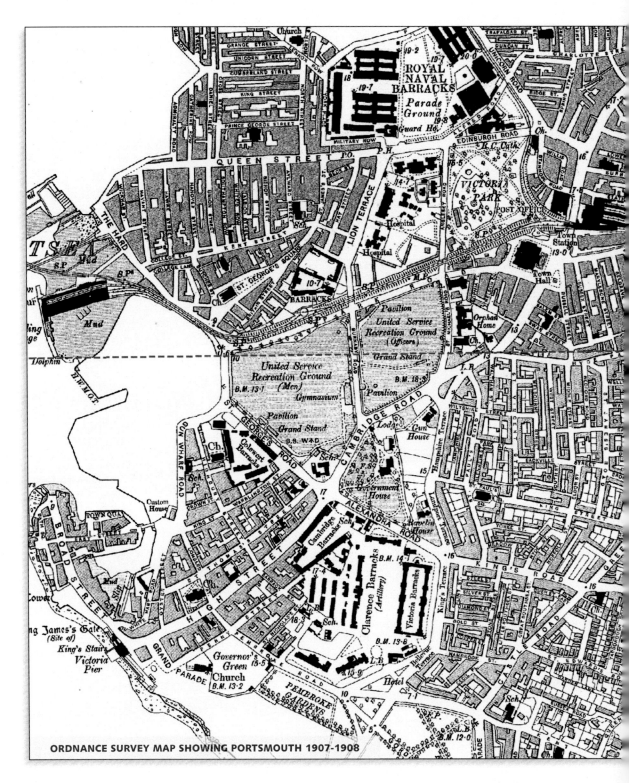

ORDNANCE SURVEY MAP SHOWING PORTSMOUTH 1907-1908

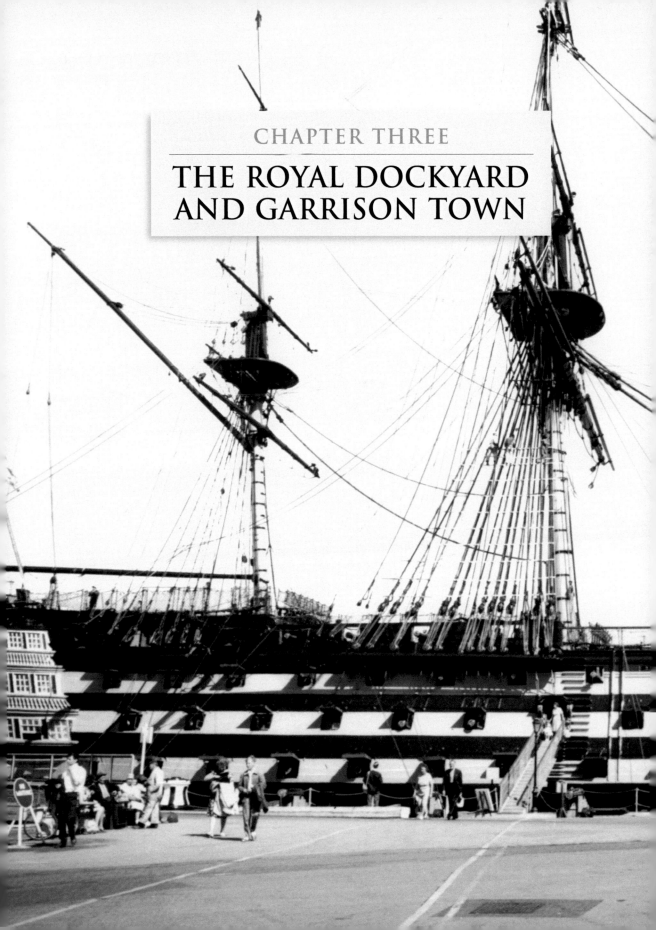

CHAPTER THREE

THE ROYAL DOCKYARD AND GARRISON TOWN

HENRY VII also designated Portsmouth a royal dockyard and garrison town, an affirmation of its importance once again to king and government. The resident garrison would protect the dockyard and related buildings, including the important victualling enterprise. Henry VIII was equally supportive. The French were still a decided threat and he needed a navy capable of offering determined resistance to the enemy. Amongst the ships which came off the building slips during the early years of his reign were the 'Mary Rose' in 1509 and, in 1510, the 'Peter Pomegranate', but, possessing a dry dock, the bulk of the work undertaken in the dockyard was repair work not ship-building.

Victualling facilities were now improved, as well. The first brewhouses were built in approximately 1492. They were 'erectid', said John Leland, by 'King Henry the vii at his firste warres into Fraunce…in the south part of the towne 3 great bruing houses with the implements to serve his shippes at such tyme as they shaul go to the se in tyme of warre'. New brewing and baking facilities were built in 1512-13. Named the Rose, the Lion, the Dragon, and the White Hart, the new brewhouses stood in St Nicholas' Street. The Great Bakehouse, called the Anchor, was in St Thomas's Street. They are all clearly marked on the 'Ancient Plan' of the town drawn later in the century in the reign of Queen Elizabeth. Their defence was a matter of some importance and considerable effort was put into throwing up a defensive ring round the town and earthworks along the shoreline when the threat of a combined invasion by the French and Spanish loomed early in 1539.

Leland described these defences. There was, he said, 'a mudde waulle armid with tymbre, wheron be great peaces both of yren, and brasen ordinauns…'. The circuit was roughly one mile. At the north-east end of the town, there was a great gate of timber and, just beyond it, said Leland, 'is cast up an hille of erth dichid', wherein be gunnes to defende entre into the town by land'.

On the seaward side of the town, the defences now ran in an unbroken line from the Round Tower as far as the present Clarence Pier and protected the harbour mouth. If a landing was attempted further east, the invaders would be met by fire from bulwarks erected to the west of South Parade Pier and to the east of Ketes Point, where Southsea Castle was later built, and even further west, by fire from yet another bulwark in the area of Lumps Fort. A bulwark was also constructed at Portsbridge to protect the bridge built originally by Richard I over Portscreek.

Leland also described the town itself at this time with its 'one fair streate' and parish church. He also noted the amount of vacant ground within the town walls, as did the young Edward VI a few years later, in 1552, on his tour of the south coast. Clearly the town had never recovered from the devastation wrought by French raiders in the late 14th century.

Southsea Castle was begun in 1544, one of a chain of similar fortifications built by Henry VIII along the south coast, possibly to his own designs. Its angled bastions represented the very latest thinking on military architecture and its guns protected the shipping channel. It was from the ramparts of Southsea Castle that the king himself watched his fleet sail out to meet a French invasion force on 18 July 1545 and saw, to his horror, his great ship, the 'Mary Rose', capsize with terrible loss of life. Fortunately, the French did not land, but the scare was sufficient to justify some further expenditure on the defences of the town. Angled bastions were erected between the Round Tower and Point Gate, by the Town Gate and 'towardes Kingeston'. A 'mounte' was built to protect the four great brewhouses, presumably like the mound erected previously by the Town Gate, and another bulwark constructed in the north-west corner of the town, known later as the Square or Dock bulwark. Little was ever done, however, to keep the town's defences in good order. The Bishop of Winchester complained bitterly about this to Cardinal

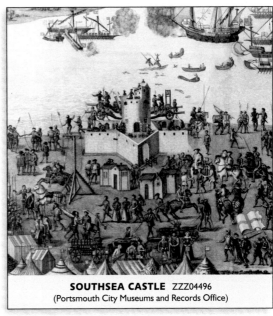

SOUTHSEA CASTLE ZZZ04496
(Portsmouth City Museums and Records Office)

This is taken from the 18th-century Cowdray Print and shows the sinking of the 'Mary Rose' in 1545.

Wolsey in 1518. 'Our maner', he said, 'is never to prepare for war to our enemies be light at our doors. Only then did we summon the fortifications to life once more.'

SOUTHSEA CASTLE 2005 S161701k (Sarah Quail)

SOUTHSEA, THE ENTRANCE TO THE CASTLE 2005 S161702k (Sarah Quail)

SOUTHSEA CASTLE

Southsea Castle represented a major shift in ideas relating to military engineering. Its construction was part of a scheme which has been described as possibly the most ambitious coastal defence project since Roman times. These new ideas originated in Italy and the eastern Mediterranean and recognised that medieval rounded towers and bastions - such as those at the harbour mouth - were too good a target for modern cannon-fire and provided too little flanking cover. Angled bastions, however, reduced the size of the target, while guns sited in the flanks of adjacent angled bastions gave all-round cover. Southsea Castle was therefore built with a square keep, rectangular gun platforms to the east and west and angled bastions on the north and south.

The governor of Portsmouth, Sir Anthony Knyvet, supervised the works with John Chaderton, the Captain of the Garrison. Construction was completed in roughly six months over the summer of 1544. Building supplies came from the Isle of Wight. Some £3,000 was expended on the project over this period, of which at least £1,300 came from the proceeds of the dissolution of the monasteries. Sir Anthony was very proud of the fact that such a fortress had never been built for so little cost.

The possibility of a Spanish attack during Queen Elizabeth's reign ensured that some work was done on the fortifications during this period. William Camden, in his survey of the British Isles called 'Britannia', published in 1586, commented both on the work done on the defences during Elizabeth's reign and on the difficulties the community always faced when any hostilities ended. Like Leland before him, he commented that Portsmouth was 'much frequented' in wartime but 'at all other times scarce at all'. Of the fortifications, he said, 'The town was anciently defended by a wall of timber covered with earth, a bastion to the north-east near the gate, and two forts of hewn stone at the mouth of the harbour, begun by Edward IV and finished by Henry VII, who placed a garrison here. But, in our time, Queen Elizabeth at great expence

fortified it so strongly with new works that nothing is wanting to make it a place of the greatest strength. Some of the garrison mount guard night and day at the gates, others in the steeple (of St Thomas's) who, by the strokes of the bell, give notice what number of horse and foot are approaching, and by a flag shew which way they come.'

The warning bell and guards at the gate are noted and remarked upon by visitors, not only in the next century but also well into the 18th century.

No further major alterations or additions were made to the fortifications until after the Restoration because although the town and dockyard were still important, they were no longer as vital to the nation's defences as they had been a century earlier. The main enemy now was the Spanish Netherlands, so that the dockyards on the Thames - Deptford, Woolwich and Chatham - were more use now to the government of the day than the dockyard on the south coast. Only when battle was joined with the new Dutch nation, and with France once more, did Portsmouth recover its position as the premier naval port and dockyard.

The town's problems were compounded by a terrible fire, which broke out in 1557 and destroyed the royal storehouse, and a particularly virulent outbreak of plague in 1563, which scythed through the local population. Efforts were made to diversify the local economy. In an attempt to encourage weaving in the town, the Queen was petitioned in 1585 to allow clothiers freedom from customs for 20 years on condition that they should each keep two corselets, ie two pieces of body armour, and able men to wear them. Official reports record that the port was, in fact, now infested with smugglers and pirates and that even the mayor was guilty of dealing with such people. There are also references to priests and recusants escaping through the port.

During the reign of James I, the dry dock was actually filled in 'to protect the dockyard from encroachments by the sea' on the orders of the king's favourite, the Duke of Buckingham, who wanted to build a replacement double dock. His assassination in 1628 by John Felton at his lodgings in the High Street put paid to these plans, though, and the town - and dockyard - was now seriously disadvantaged. Sir George Blundell described Portsmouth in 1627 as 'a poor beggarly place, where is neither money, lodging nor meat'.

Fact File

Buckingham House

The building where the Duke of Buckingham was assassinated still stands at the top of the High Street. It is known today as Buckingham House. It was known then as the Greyhound and belonged to Captain John Mason, a leading figure in the town then but better known today as one of the founders of the New England state of New Hampshire in the United States. The Greyhound was purchased in January 1705 by Dr William Smith, the garrison physician, who endowed Portsmouth Grammar School in 1732.

BUCKINGHAM HOUSE IN THE 1920s
ZZZ04497 (From Gates)

**THE MEMORIAL TO THE DUKE OF BUCKINGHAM
IN PORTSMOUTH CATHEDRAL**
ZZZ04526 (Portsmouth Cathedral)

military man, at the Governor's residence, the former Domus Dei, or God's House, and there, having raided the Governor's wine cellar, they drank '2 or 3 heartie glasses of excellent choice wine', which enabled them the better 'to march the Rounds', ie do the circuit of the town walls.

Further efforts had been made to boost the local economy when the town petitioned the king in 1625 for the renewal of their privileges and certain trading advantages. The new charter enlarged considerably those privileges granted in Elizabeth's charter of 1600, and gave the inhabitants a licence to weave, make and sell a wide range of kersies, coarse, narrow cloth, usually ribbed, and broadcloths. Slowly, the town's fortunes began to improve.

Portsmouth was engaged only briefly in the conflict when civil war broke out in 1642. Parliament was keen to secure the major ports, particularly Portsmouth. There had been rumours that Queen Henrietta Maria was in the town and that the king was on his way to join her with an army. The governor, Colonel George Goring, declared for the king, despite the fact that the town, and the population in the surrounding countryside, favoured Parliament. When Parliamentary forces took Southsea Castle without a fight, what resistance there was in Portsmouth collapsed, and Portsmouth remained loyal to Parliament for the rest of the war and during the Commonwealth. There was only one significant casualty - the parish church. St Thomas's was badly damaged by Parliamentary guns firing from the Gosport

Lieutenant Hammond, who was making a tour of the south coast in late summer 1635 was not so damning. Before he entered the town, he was struck by the 'wofull Spectacle' of Felton's bones hanging in chains, but, unabashed, he negotiated his way past the sentries and made his way to his lodgings at the Red Lion. His hostess was

'briske, blith and merry, a hansome sprightly Lasse, fit for the company of brave Commaunders: whereof there are good store, both within that Garrison Towne and the Castles there neere adioyning.'

He fell in with an acquaintance, another

side of the harbour. The medieval tower was damaged and the church was no longer fit for use. The parish decamped to the old Domus Dei until their church could be repaired.

The town may have had a relatively quiet war, but it played a key role in the events which culminated finally in the restoration of Charles II. On 26 December 1659, Civil War veteran Sir Arthur Hesilrige, Nicholas Love, one of the regicides (the men who signed the death warrant of Charles I), and Colonel Valentine Walton were admitted as burgesses of the town. Their names can still be made out in the Election Book. They had come to Portsmouth earlier in the month to rally support for a march to London to end the military dictatorship and restore the puritan republic. Their headquarters while they were in Portsmouth was the Red Lion Inn. The Corporation, whether from principle or expediency is not known, threw in their lot with Hesilrige. Portsmouth was therefore the first place in England to rebel against military government and therefore played a significant part in the events which led to the restoration of the king. The restoration of the king did, in fact, leave Portsmouth in something of a quandary, as the town had declared originally for the republic, but while there were without doubt men in Portsmouth loyal to the ideals of the republic, there were others who were fairly indifferent to the actual form of government, as long as it gave them the stability they needed to ply their trades profitably.

The king promised forgiveness for all but the regicides and the names of Hesilrige,

Love and Walton were expunged from the Election Book. A group of 'loyalists' were admitted in their place. There were further opportunities to demonstrate commitment to the new order when the king's bride, the Portuguese princess, Catherine of Braganza, landed at Portsmouth on 14 May 1662. The marriage took place in due course in the Governor's residence, the old Domus Dei, as the parish church was still in ruins. A loyal address and speech of welcome from the mayor and a very handsome gift of a salt cellar for the bride and groom smoothed over any embarrassments there may have been - and the king contributed, in due course, to the appeal to rebuild the parish church.

CHARLES II'S MARRIAGE CERTIFICATE, WITH THE EARLY PARISH REGISTERS c1925
ZZZ04527 (Portsmouth Cathedral)

THE ROYAL DOCKYARD AND GARRISON TOWN

Samuel Pepys remarked on the beauty of the gift. He was in Portsmouth in late April 1662 in the large official party awaiting the imminent arrival of the Portuguese royal party. It was, he said, 'a salt-sellar of silver, the walls of cristall, with four Eagles and four greyhounds standing up at top to bear up a dish - which endeed is one of the neatest pieces of plate that ever I saw.'

On another visit, almost twelve months previously, he too stayed at the Red Lion, where, he noted, Hesilrige, Love and Walton stayed in December 1659. The Red Lion stood at the junction of the High Street and Church Lane, which no longer exists but then ran between the High Street and St Thomas's Street, skirting the end of the parish church. It is covered now by Sir Charles Nicholson's extensions to the cathedral undertaken in the 1930s. Parts of the inn yard and some footings were discovered again recently in an archaeological survey of land adjacent to Michael Drury's most recent extension. Pepys used this particular occasion in 1661 to visit the room in the building at the top of the High Street where the Duke of Buckingham was killed by Felton. Clearly, memories of this infamous event still haunted the ruling classes.

The Parliamentarians had recognised the importance of naval power and there was renewed interest in the dockyard in the late 1640s and 1650s, which the long series of wars, first against the Dutch and later against the French in the late Stuart and Georgian periods, only increased. Much work came to the dockyard, which was extended significantly on at least three separate occasions over the next two hundred years. A new building slip was completed in 1649, and in the 1650s a new - double - dry dock was built, together with a mast wharf and tar house, and a small, one-and-a-half acre plot was laid out as a rope yard. The first Dutch War of 1652-4, far from diverting activity to the Thames yards, only confirmed Portsmouth's growing strategic importance once more, because the Channel was a vital sea-lane for Dutch colonial traffic.

The expansion of the dockyard continued after the Restoration and during the 2nd and 3rd Dutch Wars of 1665-7 and 1672-4. Money was voted for a new dry dock in 1662 and a huge, thousand-foot-long wooden rope house was completed in 1663 on an eight-acre strip of land to the south of the yard. A mast pond was completed in 1666. Besides providing ship-repair facilities, Portsmouth also became a leading ship-building yard. There were useful supplies of timber nearby in the Forest of Bere and eighteen ships were built between 1660 and 1674, including two first-rate ones of one hundred guns, the 'Royal James' and the 'Royal Charles'. The first ship to have its bottom sheathed with lead to protect it from the dreaded boring worm, terredo navalis, the 5th-rate 'Phoenix', was launched in Portsmouth in 1671.

The town's fortifications were also improved significantly during the reign of Charles II. Soon after the king returned, he initiated a major review of the nation's defences and, over the next 20 years or so, the defences of the more important naval ports and dockyards, opposite the French and Dutch coasts, were brought up to date. Work began in Portsmouth, in 1665, to the designs of Sir Bernard de Gomme, the king's chief engineer. Sir Bernard was a Netherlander who had given distinguished service on the royalist side during the Civil War. Clearly, he was familiar with developments in the theory of fortification in the 17th century in both his own country and in France. The emphasis of defence was moving away from defending the curtain walls of strongholds outwards, beyond any original moat, to additional moats or water barriers and outworks. The original line of the ramparts was retained in Portsmouth, but a major rebuild took place, and the defences were pushed out to a second moat and the necessary related outworks. The dockyard itself was enclosed with an earth rampart, topped by a wooden palisade, with an east-facing and a south-facing bastion. At Southsea Castle, the defences were strengthened with a dry moat, glacis and covered way. The works took 20 years to complete. By the time they were finished, Portsmouth had one of the most impressive defensive systems in Europe and was probably the most powerful citadel in the kingdom with the largest concentration of troops outside London.

The king died in 1685. His marriage to Catherine of Braganza had been childless and he was succeeded by his brother, the Roman Catholic James and, as they had done during the last days of the Commonwealth, the people of Portsmouth now played a key role once again on the national stage in the weeks between the invasion of Prince William of Orange and the flight of James II. The catalyst was a mutiny among local army officers. This was the affair of the 'Portsmouth Captains' who refused to absorb large numbers of Irish recruits into the garrison. These events have to be seen against a background of mounting tension and anti-Catholic sentiment in the country as James pursued his plans for a Declaration of Indulgence and the repeal of the penal laws and Test Act. James claimed to be doing this in the name of liberty of conscience and equality of rights, but his subjects saw his actions as a plot to subvert Protestantism and our national institutions and hand them over to Catholics. The propaganda machine of the king's enemies went to work. The regiments brought over by James from Ireland were overwhelmingly Catholic and the foot soldiers native Irish. Religious paranoia and racial bigotry were exploited brilliantly.

The six 'Portsmouth Captains' were put on trial in London. They quickly became national heroes. In his efforts to defuse the situation, the king just dismissed them from army service but back in Portsmouth, events rapidly got out of hand. There were massive concentrations of troops in the town as fears of invasion increased. The men were billeted on the local population and, like most 17th-century armies, they were ill-disciplined, violent and predatory.

There were widespread incidents reported of robbery, drunkenness and affray. Most sensational of all was an incident in late October 1688, when some Irishmen fired bullets into the parish church during divine service. Many were either killed or wounded. The diarist, John Evelyn, noted in his diary that the king 'continues to remove Protestants and put papists into Portsmouth and other places of trust…'. Such activities gave credence to rumours now circulating that Queen Mary and the infant Prince of Wales were about to leave London and take up residence near Portsmouth, a fortress into which they could retreat, if need be, and there arrange their passages out of the country. Other rumours had it that the king planned to arrest his enemies and imprison them, not in the Tower of London, but at Portsmouth.

The Prince of Wales was brought to Portsmouth and lodged briefly in Alderman Ridge's house in the High Street, which was generally acknowledged to be the grandest house in the town. By this time, however, support for the king was ebbing fast. William of Orange had landed at Tor Bay and was marching towards London. Portsmouth was in chaos and there was open fighting on the streets between different groups of soldiers and sailors. Support for the king from the fleet, and its commander, Lord Dartmouth, evaporated. Urged by royal officials to press local men to prepare the defences for action, the mayor fled instead to the safety of Lord Dartmouth's flagship, followed closely by Alderman Ridge.

The king now sent his illegitimate son, the Duke of Berwick, to Portsmouth to take personal command of the town, but before he arrived, the king had fled, and Lord Dartmouth and the fleet now came

over openly to William of Orange. However, Portsmouth's situation did not improve immediately. There were now hundreds of disaffected troops, many Irish, dismissed from their regiments and roaming the town and surrounding countryside. The situation was saved by the redoubtable Civil War veteran, Colonel Richard Norton of Southwick, who raised the country for ten miles round Portsmouth, assembled a force of a thousand horse and foot on the top of Portsdown and thus prevented anyone getting either in or out of Portsmouth. Finally, to the relief of the residents, on the evening of 20 December 1688, the new garrison of Prince William's men arrived. In due course, barracks were built to accommodate troops, thus relieving the long-suffering local population of the hated imposition of billeted men. By the mid 18th century, three separate barrack blocks, capable of accommodating 380 men, had been constructed.

By the end of the 17th century, Portsmouth was not only the most powerful citadel in the kingdom, but it was also the country's leading naval dockyard, following the completion of the dock-building programme begun in 1689, which doubled the size of the dockyard to 28 acres. The first naval stone dock had been completed behind an enclosed basin, where ships could be refitted more easily than at anchor in the harbour. An innovatory pumping system which used horse-power was installed to drain dock and basin quickly and easily. A second rope house of similar size to the first was also constructed and the Great Long Storehouse next to it. The number of men employed in the dockyard rose significantly during the reigns of William and Mary, and William III. In 1687, there was a workforce of 294 men. By 1697, there were 1,271 and by 1711, 2,000. With the end of hostilities in 1713, the numbers dropped to 1,200, but Portsmouth dockyard was still the largest manufacturing enterprise in the country and would remain so until the mid 19th century.

Daniel Defoe took stock of the town in 1724. He was impressed by the strength of the defences round the town. 'The works', he said, 'are very large and numerous', and benefited now from 'the fortifications raised in King William's time about the docks and yards… The town,' he wrote, 'besides its being a fortification, is a well inhabited, thriving, prosperous corporation; and hath been greatly enrich'd of late by the fleet's having so often and so long lain there, as well as large fleets of merchant-men, as the whole navy during the late war; besides the constant fitting out of men there, and the often paying them at Portsmouth, has made a great confluence of people thither…these things have not only been a great advantage to the town, but has really made the whole place rich, and the inhabitants of Portsmouth are quite another sort of people than they were a few years before the Revolution; this is what Mr Cambden (William Camden) takes

THE LANDPORT GATE, ERECTED 1760 ZZZ04498 (From Gates)

THE ROYAL DOCKYARD AND GARRISON TOWN

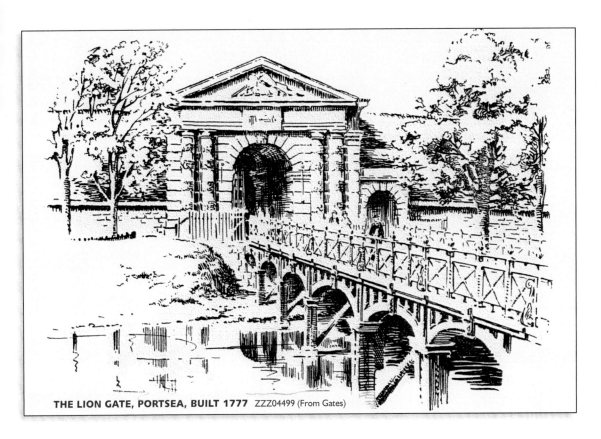

THE LION GATE, PORTSEA, BUILT 1777 ZZZ04499 (From Gates)

UNICORN GATE, PORTSEA, ERECTED 1778-9 ZZZ04500 (From Gates)

notice of, even so long ago as the reign of Queen Elizabeth.'

The disadvantages of living in a garrison town 'such as being examin'd at the gates, such as being obliged to keep garrison hours, and not be let out, or let in after nine a clock at night, and the like' counted for little, he reckoned, when you got your living 'by the very situation of the place, as is the case here'.

The town's fortunes did fluctuate, but despite the changing circumstances of peace and war throughout the long series of wars against France in the 18th and early 19th centuries, including the American Revolutionary War, the numbers of dockyard workers continued to rise. By the mid 18th century, there were 2,000 men once again, by 1800 almost 3,000 and by 1814, almost 4,000.

A major modernization and redevelopment of dockyard facilities took place on the accession of George III in 1760. More building slips were laid out and a second stone dock was constructed giving into the basin. Work also began replacing the old timber storehouses and rope houses with brick buildings less prone to the scourge of fire. A new double rope house was built in brick in 1770 on the site of the two old rope houses, one of which had been destroyed by fire. French and Spanish agents were believed to have been the culprits then. A tarring house and a hatchelling house, where the hemp fibres were carded, were built, too. Most of these magnificent brick buildings have survived and are at the heart of today's historic dockyard and heritage attraction. The brick storehouses are the home today of the Royal Naval Museum.

Besides these essentially industrial buildings, other domestic and institutional buildings were constructed in the dockyard during the 18th century. Long Row was built in 1717 to house senior naval officers of the dockyard establishment. It was much

'JACK THE PAINTER'

James Aitken, or 'Jack the Painter' - he trained as a house-painter - was hanged just outside the gates of Portsmouth Dockyard on 10 March 1777, reputedly on the highest gallows ever erected in England. He was only 25 years old. He was an impassioned supporter of the principles of the American Revolution and has been described latterly as the first British terrorist, someone who committed acts of terror in this country on behalf of a foreign power.

His first act of terror was to try and burn down Portsmouth Dockyard in late 1776, but only the recently reconstructed ropehouse was destroyed. He decamped in the early months of 1777 to Bristol, where he tried, with varying degrees of success, to destroy several merchant ships, warehouses and the homes of prominent citizens. The nation was panicstricken. It was believed that a team of arsonists was on the loose and ready to strike anywhere and at any time. The king and most of his ministers were aghast. Habeas Corpus was suspended and Sir John Fielding, London's famous magistrate, was asked to advise on what to do for the best. He recommended a large reward and, within barely a week, 'Jack the Painter' was apprehended and sent shortly afterwards to the gallows.

altered, however, in the early 19th century, when the brick facades were covered in stucco and porches were added. The Royal Naval Academy was built in 1729-32 to prepare boys for the navy. It is regarded as the best 18th-century building in the city today. Admiralty House, next door, was built in 1784-6 for the Admiralty Commissioner for the Dockyard to the designs of James Wyatt's brother, Samuel. Thomas Telford, as a young man, supervised the building of Admiralty House. He also supervised the rebuilding of the dockyard church of St Ann, built originally in 1704, and is believed to have designed Short Row, a terrace of six houses built in 1787 for important civilian dockyard officials. Most of these buildings are used today for office accommodation, but Admiralty House is still an official residence - of the Second Sea Lord.

By the 1790s, there was a serious need for more and better ship-repair and refit facilities and the Navy Board invited Samuel Bentham to suggest how more efficient working practices might best be achieved. He observed that a lot of time - and money - was lost by the shipwrights in getting out to the ships on which they were working at anchor in the harbour, and suggested that the basin should be enlarged, that two more dry docks, giving into the basin, should be built, that the old double dock and South Dock should be dismantled and a new dock, with access to the harbour, be constructed. His proposals were accepted and, under his supervision as Inspector-General of Naval Works, they were completed by 1803.

Bentham utilised the reservoir of the drainage system introduced to drain the docks and basin in the late 17th century, but introduced a steam engine in place of horse power to pump the water out of the reservoir. It was the first steam engine installed in the dockyard. In due course, steam power would revolutionise working life there.

Not long afterwards, Bentham persuaded the Navy Board - again in the interests of efficiency and economy - to instal Marc Isambard Brunel's pulley-block-making machinery in the dockyard. A block is the pulley mechanism which takes the strain

Fact File

Portsmouth's Scarlet Pimpernel

An unlikely clandestine figure, the Reverend Thomas Wren, the minister at the Presbyterian Chapel in the High Street, also supported the ideals of the American Revolution, and when a prison was set up for captured American seamen at Forton in 1777, he paid regular visits to the captives, taking with him donations from other local sympathisers. It is also clear, from the surviving diaries of prisoners, that he facilitated a number of escapes, despite the risks involved, gave the men sanctuary in his chapel and sent them on their way to safe houses in London where they could usually find passages to France. After the peace, in appreciation of his kindness and generosity, the American Congress passed a vote of thanks to Mr Wren. He resumed his normal ministry and died peacefully in Portsmouth in 1787.

of a rope in a ship's rigging. It was a vital piece of equipment. A large ship such as HMS 'Victory' needed at least 1,000 blocks, and the Navy purchased some 100,000 each year, in the main from the Taylor family at Swaythling, near Southampton.

Brunel had taken out a patent on his design for a steam-driven block-making machine in 1801 and had made models of these designs. He had tried to interest the Taylors in his ideas, but they could not be persuaded to adopt them. However, Bentham was interested and Brunel's pulley-block-making machinery was installed in Portsmouth dockyard. The block mills building was the first steam-powered factory in a British naval dockyard. There were 45 machines and they were the first examples in the world of the use of metal machines for mass production. By 1805, the new machinery was producing all the blocks needed. Other innovations of Bentham's included the provision of a water tank on the roof of the block mills as a firefighting precaution, the erection of a water tower near the rope house for similar reasons and the building of a steam dredger for clearing the basin. This must be the piece of equipment, or one very similar to it, described by a fascinated visitor to the dockyard in 1807.

The writer 'stood some time admiring the construction of a piece of machinery in the harbour, formed for clearing away mud. Two vessels lie close together, and in one a circular chain revolves by means of steam, each link having iron buckets, so sharp and narrow at the edge, as to scoop up a quantity of mud at every descent; and, carrying this to the top

Fact File

Isambard Kingdom Brunel

Marc Isambard Brunel was the father of the great 19th-century engineer, Isambard Kingdom Brunel. Marc and his wife, Sophia, lived not far from the dockyard in Britain Street, Portsea, where their son was born on 9 April 1806. He was christened at St Mary's, Portsea.

THE HOUSE IN WHICH ISAMBARD KINGDOM BRUNEL IS BELIEVED TO HAVE BEEN BORN
ZZZ04501 (From Gates)

of their ascent, they deposit it, on revolving, in a long wooden channel placed obliquely, and reaching to the other boat, into which, of course, the mud slides of itself.'

The work carried on in the dockyard

and later, HMS 'Victory', and the fact that Portsmouth was a fortified town with a military guard were of abiding interest to visitors to the town. Road travel became easier as the 18th century progressed and roads improved. As a result, there were more visitors to the town and the number of descriptions increase. The view of Portsea Island from the top of Portsdown Hill captivated many travellers. The Reverend William Gilpin, a New Forest clergyman, made a tour of Hampshire, Sussex and Kent in 1774 and penned the first full description of the view:

'From the top of Portsdown-hill, where we soon arrived, we had a view grander in its kind than perhaps any part of the globe can exhibit. Beneath our feet lay a large extent of marshy ground, which is covered with water when the tides flow high, and adorned with innumerable islands and peninsulas. About a mile from the eye, this marsh is joined by the isle of Portsea, distinguished by its peculiar fertility, and the luxuriance of its woods; among which the town of Portsmouth appears to rise at the distance of five miles… . The harbour of Portsmouth, which would contain all the shipping in Europe, was the grand feature of this view. Besides innumerable skiffs and smaller vessels plying about this ample basin, we counted between fifty and sixty sail of the line. Some of them appeared lying unrigged on the water; others in commission with their colours flying. Beyond Portsmouth we had a view of the sea, which is generally crowded with ships…where some men of war are commonly waiting for the wind.'

But it was the fortified enclave and the dockyard itself which most fascinated visitors.

William Gilpin was no exception. 'Portsmouth, he declared, with all its gates, its ditches, bastions, batteries, and other works, is a new sight to a traveller who has never seen a fortified town or a naval arsenal. The bakery, salting-houses, and other victualling offices would appear enormous, if we had not a counterpart in the many floating castles and towns lying ready in the harbours to receive their contents…'

Thomas Pennant, the antiquary and naturalist, travelling to the Isle of Wight in 1793, just before the outbreak of the Napoleonic Wars, described the place where the anchors were made as 'truly a giant's cave: seventy or eighty brawny fellows were amidst the fires busied in fabricating those securities to our shipping'. As for the rope-walk, it was, he said, 'not less than eight hundred and seventy feet long. The making a great cable is a wonderful sight; a hundred men are required for the purpose, and the labour is so hard that they cannot work at it more than four hours in the day.' The vastness of the magazines, he reckoned, 'can scarcely be conceived'.

Joseph Haydn visited Portsmouth in July 1794 and was equally impressed by the sheer scale of the enterprise that was Portsmouth Dockyard. He was on a visit at the time to London and had seen the great excitement which greeted the news of Lord Howe's victory of the Glorious First of June, and resolved to go down to Portsmouth to see for himself the French prizes at anchor. He inspected the fortifications and actually went on board one of the French prizes, which, he recorded in his notebook, was 'terribly shot to pieces'. 'The dockyard, or the place where ships are built,' he wrote, 'is of an enormous size, and has a great many splendid buildings'. But, sadly, he was not allowed to enter the dockyard because he was 'a foreigner'. The artist J M W Turner was equally captivated by these things, and even more so by the wind and weather, particularly the misty atmosphere

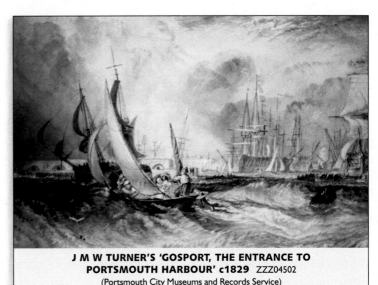

J M W TURNER'S 'GOSPORT, THE ENTRANCE TO PORTSMOUTH HARBOUR' c1829 ZZZ04502
(Portsmouth City Museums and Records Service)

of the town. Views of Portsmouth produced by Turner have been compared with his late watercolours of Venice.

J M W TURNER

The artist J M W Turner visited Portsmouth on several occasions between 1807 and 1844, and in the Turner bequest at Tate Britain in London, a series of sketchbooks survives, in which Turner recorded these visits. He used the sketches to work up pictures later, back in his London studio. His first fully documented visit to Portsmouth took place in early November 1807 and, from the studies he made which survive in the 'Spithead' sketchbook, he produced the picture known today as 'Spithead: Boat's Crew Recovering an Anchor'. He was in Portsmouth again in 1814, when the Allied Sovereigns visited the town. The 'Review at Portsmouth' sketchbook contains a wealth of detail of Portsmouth's shoreline observed from the sea. Southsea Castle, the Saluting Platform, the Round Tower, St Thomas's, Gunwharf and the dockyard, all are identifiable in Turner's sketches. Turner also produced three watercolours of Portsmouth at this time, to be engraved for his landscape series, 'Southern Coast', 'Ports of England' and 'Picturesque Views in England and Wales'. Portsmouth City Museums and Records Service owns the watercolour view of the harbour that Turner painted in 1829-30 for 'Picturesque Views'.

His last visit, in 1844, took place when he was nearly 65. He came to see the arrival in Portsmouth of King Louis-Philippe of France on a state visit to this country. In the Turner Bequest, a series of sketches survives which were clearly produced during this visit, but it was not thought that he worked the sketches up into anything more significant until, very recently, a pair of pictures thought to be of Venice were reattributed to Portmouth!

By the 1830s, the coal-fired steam engine had arrived in the dockyard and steamship construction was underway. Another visitor to the dockyard, George Simson, a tax surveyor of Hereford, who kept a detailed diary of a holiday trip to the Isle of Wight in 1839, noted these developments: 'After dinner we went by steamer to Portsmouth and forthwith to the Dock Yard. Much pleased with the Mast Stores - Timber Stores - sawing machinery, making of the Blocks, saw one made throughout - pleased with the furnace for melting copper drawing the iron out - the whole done by Steam Power.'

The first steamship, the 'Neptune', was launched in 1832. The advantages of screw propulsion over the paddle, discovered in 1840, accelerated the move from sail to steam. The new trades of boilermaker, engineer, fitter and foundryman existed now alongside the historic dockyard skills and by 1850, the dockyard workforce was almost back to the Napoleonic War levels of nearly 4,000 men.

The dockyard was extended again, first in the 1840s when a new steam basin was constructed on land reclaimed from the sea, and again in the 1860s - the Great Extension - when the area occupied by the yard trebled in size from 99 to 261 acres.

Half of this new acreage was claimed from the sea, the rest came from the area cleared by the demolition of the now redundant Portsea defences. The expansion was driven in great part by fears of war once again with France. The French ironclad, 'La Gloire', was a new breed of warship, seemingly invincible. The 1840 extensions were not adequate to cope with this new technology. The new interconnected basins had a combined area of 52 acres. They can still be observed by today's holidaymakers from the decks of the cross-channel ferries manoeuvring in and out of their berths at Portsmouth's Continental Ferry Port. Work on the new basin, its five docks and adjacent workshops, was completed in 1881. It was the last great territorial expansion of the naval dockyard. Only minor modifications, by comparison, took place to docks and basins in the 1890s and early 20th century.

It was fear of war with France, the possibility of invasion and misgivings generally about the adequacy of the nation's defences which prompted Lord Palmerston's government to

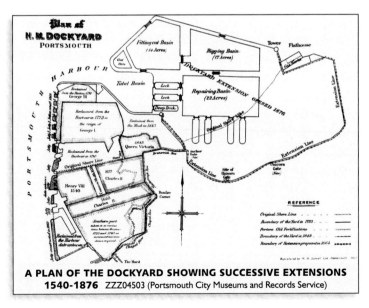

A PLAN OF THE DOCKYARD SHOWING SUCCESSIVE EXTENSIONS 1540-1876 ZZZ04503 (Portsmouth City Museums and Records Service)

appoint a royal commission to investigate their state. The commission began work in 1859 and reported within the year. There was a great deal of opposition to the proposals in parliament. Many members felt that the Prime Minister was over-reacting to an exaggerated threat and, in the course of one angry exchange between him and his Chancellor of the Exchequer, Mr Gladstone, the former opined that if it came to a choice, it would be better to lose Mr Gladstone, who was threatening to resign, than to lose Portsmouth.

The Commissioners recommended that the dockyard, which they acknowledged was by now the most important in the British Isles, and the anchorage at Spithead should have better protection, given the recent significant developments in the range and effectiveness of artillery. What this meant, in practical terms, was that the defensible area round Portsmouth and its dockyard needed now to be pushed out at least as far as the Needles Passage and Portsdown Hill; work, therefore, began on building a ring of forts round Portsmouth. The project took over 20 years to complete, by which time the threat from France had disappeared, but for a while Portsmouth was one of the most heavily defended places in the world. The string of forts on top of Portsdown Hill - Wallington, Nelson, Southwick, Widley, Purbrook and Farlington - faced north deliberately in order to repudiate an enemy force which might have landed further along the coast and attempted to surprise the town from the north. The sea forts of iron and granite built

on shoals at Spitbank, Horse Sand, No Man's Land and St Helen's, defended the Spithead anchorage, the harbour and its entrance. It was the last great defensive scheme carried out in the Portsmouth area. Minor works were carried out to the existing defences up to, and including, the two world wars, but no new works were undertaken.

The growth of the dockyard and the need for more workers put pressure on available accommodation from the mid 17th century. Initially, the low-lying shingle spit of Portsmouth Point, curving round the Camber at the harbour entrance, was encroached upon. It was accessed through Point Gate, known later as King James Gate, at the bottom of the High Street. There were only two houses and limekilns on the spit in the late 16th century, but, by the mid 17th century, it was a well-developed suburb with more than its fair share of taverns, inns and lodging houses and it had a lively reputation. But there were respectable residents there: sail- and rope-makers, dealers of every description, dockyard workers, watermen and ferrymen.

There was a limit, though, to how many people could be housed on the Point and within the confines of the town itself so, early in the 18th century, houses began to be built outside the walls to the north, on Portsmouth Common, and on the East and West Dock Fields, part of the ancient common-field system belonging to the original 12th-century settlement. The new suburb developed rapidly. Daniel Defoe noted these developments at the time of his visit in 1724:

THE ROYAL DOCKYARD AND GARRISON TOWN

'Since the encrease of business at this place, by the long continuance of the war, the confluence of people has been so great, and the town not admitting any enlargement for buildings, that a kind of a suburb or rather a new town has been built on the healthy ground adjoining to the town, which is so well built, and seems to encrease so fast, that in time it threatens to outdo for numbers of inhabitants, and beauty of buildings, even the town itself.'

By 1753, the inhabitants of this new town were numerous enough to raise sufficient funds to build St George's Church as a chapel-of-ease to the parish church of St Mary's, Portsea, over a mile away. A second church, St John's, also a chapel-of-ease, was built

in 1787 to minister to the needs of the burgeoning population. In 1770, the fortification of both the new town and the neighbouring dockyard began. Ramparts were built, similar to those constructed by de Gomme round the old town. Two gates, the Lion and the Unicorn gates, pierced the ramparts. Both gates survive to this day. The Lion Gate was built into the base of Semaphore Tower in the dockyard in 1926-9 and the Unicorn Gate stands just inside today's main gate to the Naval Base.

Prosperity was fitful, of course, and reflected the vicissitudes of war and peace. The sums spent on poor relief, for example, spiralled when men were laid off in the dockyard, but fortunes were made in the boom

'PORTSMOUTH POINT' BY THOMAS ROWLANDSON c1800 ZZZ04504 (Portsmouth City Museums and Records Service)

war years by local tradesman and merchants, many of whom were local aldermen. In fact, the judicious administration of naval and military contracts by the government ensured that for much of the 18th century, the borough and its parliamentary seats sat snugly in its grasp. In 1792, the new suburb at last acquired its own name of Portsea. By the time the first census took place in 1801, Portsea was over three times as large as Portsmouth. The population of the parish of Portsmouth was 7,839 and that of the parish of Portsea, 24,327.

There are many lively accounts of what it was like in the two towns when ships were preparing to go to sea, or when they returned from long voyages and victorious campaigns. Thomas Rowlandson's famous cartoon 'Portsmouth Point' c1800 captures the atmosphere vividly and inspired Sir William Walton's lively overture of the same name in 1925. Dr George Pinckard's dyspeptic account of the time he spent in Portsmouth in autumn 1795 is as good an account as any of late 18th-century Portsmouth. As so many commentators have noted before him, the busy activity of the place occurs only at intervals, as when a fleet comes in or is about to sail, at which periods the town becomes all crowd and hurry for a few days and then suddenly reverts to a languid intermission of dullness and inactivity.

He also notes that the rent of houses and apartments, and the cost of provisions, differed markedly in times of peace and war. They had their war price and their peace price, distinctly fixed. Portsmouth itself, he said, was not unlike other towns, but Point, Portsea and other parts of the growing conurbation had 'peculiarities which seem to sanction the celebrity the place has acquired': 'In some quarters Portsmouth is not only filthy, and crowded, but crowded with a class of low and abandoned beings, who seem to have declared open war against every habit of common decency and decorum…The riotous, drunken, and immoral scenes of this place, perhaps exceed all others. Commonly gross obscenity and intoxification preserve enough of diffidence to seek the concealment of night…but hordes of profligate females are seen reeling in drunkenness, or plying upon the streets in open day with a broad immodesty which puts the great orb of noon to the blush… .'

He captures magnificently the frenetic atmosphere - the 'extreme hurry and activity' - of the place in the days before a fleet sailed. Shops were emptied of their goods. Not a loaf, a piece of meat, a carrot or a cabbage was to be had, and multitudes of anxious, heavily-laden individuals could be seen running with their purchase down to the boats for all the world as if the entire local population was attempting to carry off its possessions before evacuating the town to an enemy. He remarked on the legs and shoulders of mutton, half a sheep, huge pieces of beef and pork, cheeses and a sugar-loaf being lifted into craft with bread, baskets of greens and potatoes. Other people were weighed down with heavy loads of clothes, still damp from the wash, camp stools, deal boxes, sea-chests, and the like, and the general confusion was compounded by disputes and quarrels, the sadness of partings, the cries of friends greeting each other or meeting unexpectedly and sailors quitting their trolls; drunkards reeling; boatmen wrangling; boats overloaded or upset; the tide beating in heavy spray upon the shore; persons running and hurrying in every direction for something new or something forgot; some cursing the boatmen for not pushing off with more speed and others beseeching and imploring them to stop a minute longer.

Conditions changed little in the ten years or so between Dr Pinckard's commentary and that of the unknown gentleman who wrote so enthusiastically about the new steam dredger in 1807. The streets were still 'uncleanly' and 'wretched' and the sailors still had their 'trolls' on their arms 'decked out in flaring ribbons'. He describes the alehouses 'with a pas de deux between Jack and a Portsmouth Parisot, in the vestibule, to the elegant strains of two blind fiddlers', and lively scenes in the coffee houses 'where every table is covered with fierce cocked hats and hangers; and where every five minutes you hear - 'Waiter! Get me a beef-steak; and bear a hand'.

Inns and alehouses were not the only sources of entertainment. There were ready audiences in the town in the large numbers of naval and military men, whether based there temporarily or more permanently, for a wide range of dramatic and musical entertainment. Plays were performed in a local inn, the Queen's Head, from at least the late 17th century, and there appears to have been a playhouse in Highbury Street by the early 18th century. The earliest theatre which we

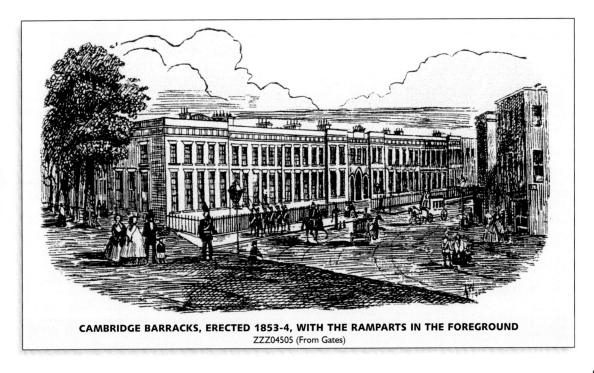

CAMBRIDGE BARRACKS, ERECTED 1853-4, WITH THE RAMPARTS IN THE FOREGROUND
ZZZ04505 (From Gates)

can be confident about was at the top of the High Street, opposite Portsmouth Grammar School's present frontage. It was leased for many years to reputable London and provincial companies. In 1761, a rival theatre was built on the opposite side of the street and remained in use until 1854, when it was demolished to make way for a new extension to the Cambridge Barracks, now occupied by the Portsmouth Grammar School. It was this theatre which was immortalised by Charles Dickens in 'Nicholas Nickleby'. During their existence, some of the most famous theatrical names of the day appeared in these theatres, including Mrs Siddons and Mrs Jordan.

Ad hoc musical entertainment was undoubtedly to be found wherever people gathered and beer was served. Organised popular musical entertainment may well have been available from the late 18th century at the Sadler's Wells, established 1781-3, which stood in today's Guildhall Walk, whether on the site of the New Theatre Royal built in 1884 is not clear. However, in the course of the 19th century and well into the 20th century, a succession of theatres and music halls in the Landport area catered not only for the large numbers of soldiers and sailors in the town but for the increasing numbers of local residents.

For more fastidious tastes, there were concerts of sacred music by visiting singers and instrumentalists from the late 18th century. Stephen Sibley and his son, Edward, were responsible for organising subscription concerts for almost half a century. From 1801, they provided local audiences with some of the finest performers available in the country. Handel's oratorios were particularly popular. Efforts were even made to establish a music festival, a three-day event similar to the Three Choirs Festival. Artists engaged to sing by the Siblys included Madam Catalini, who was regarded as one of the best singers in the world when she sang at a concert featuring a selection of sacred music from The Messiah and items by Haydn, and Pergolesi, Gulielmi, Leo and others, in St Paul's Church, Southsea on 25 August 1824 during the Music Festival.

Franz Liszt performed in Portsmouth in August 1840. Other internationally renowned performers brought to Portsmouth included Niccolo Paganini and Johann Strauss the elder, for not all the concerts promoted were 'classical'. Songs from oratorios, lieder and lighter items, such as glees, elegies and ballads, interspersed symphonies, concertos and sonatas. Besides local churches, concert venues included the Beneficial Society's Hall in Portsea, the Green Row Rooms in Portsmouth and the local theatres.

ST PAUL'S CHAPEL 1823 ZZZ04506
(Portsmouth City Museums and Records Service)

THE ROYAL DOCKYARD AND GARRISON TOWN

News of famous victories often reached Portsmouth first and naval heroes such as Lord Howe, Earl St Vincent and Lord Nelson were feted enthusiastically by local crowds on their arrival and departure. Lord Howe was received 'amidst the loudest acclamations' when he arrived back in Portsmouth on 15 June 1794 following his defeat of the French fleet on 1st June. Ten days later, George III, the Queen, Prince Ernest Augustus and two of the Princesses came down to Portsmouth and received the hero. Miss Louisa Howe and Miss Mary Howe were great friends of the Princess Royal and the younger Princesses, so there was particular royal interest in this expedition to Portsmouth.

Royal visits were not exceptional. George III had made an extensive tour of the dockyard, the fortifications and the fleet in 1773. On this occasion, he launched the second-rate battleship the Prince of Wales. George IV, William IV and Queen Victoria all visited Portsmouth on a number of occasions. Queen Victoria first visited the town as a girl with her mother, the Duchess of Kent, in 1831. In her long reign, she came to Portsmouth many times, either on her way to Osborne House on the Isle of Wight or on official business - to visit or to review the fleet, or to welcome visiting monarchs and heads of foreign states to this country. She died at Osborne on 22 January 1901. On 1 February, her coffin was borne on the royal yacht along the Solent past a long line of British and foreign warships firing minute guns into Portsmouth Harbour. Thousands watched the yacht's passage from the neighbouring shores.

QUEEN VICTORIA'S COFFIN BEING BORNE ON THE ROYAL YACHT FROM THE ISLE OF WIGHT TO PORTSMOUTH 1901 ZZZ04507 (Portsmouth City Museums and Records Service)

One of the most spectacular gatherings of royalty and heads of state in the early 19th century took place in Portsmouth between 22 and 25 June 1814 on the occasion of the visit of the Allied Sovereigns to mark what they believed was the conclusion of hostilities against Napoleonic France. The Prince Regent, the Duke of Cambridge, the King of Prussia, the Emperor of Russia, the Duke of Wellington and Marshal Blucher, with their courts and retinues, were present in Portsmouth for, between them, four days and, in company with thousands of enthusiastic local people and other visitors, gave themselves up to a feast of celebrations: levees, balls, dinners, suppers and tours of the fleet and dockyard. The streets and many of the major properties in Portsmouth were illuminated, to the wonder

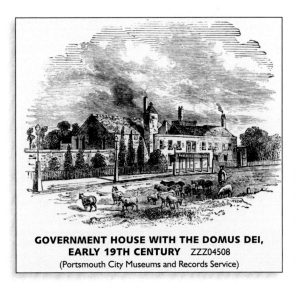

GOVERNMENT HOUSE WITH THE DOMUS DEI, EARLY 19TH CENTURY ZZZ04508
(Portsmouth City Museums and Records Service)

and delight of the crowds. The word 'Peace', flanked by stars, laurel, and crowns, expressed in coloured lamps on the front of Government House, was particularly admired.

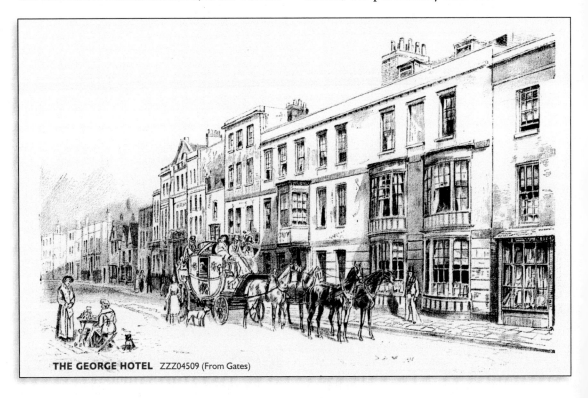

THE GEORGE HOTEL ZZZ04509 (From Gates)

A vast throng of local people gathered on the westernmost end of Southsea beach to bid farewell to Lord Nelson when he left England for the last time on 14 September 1805. He breakfasted at the George Hotel in the High Street, but the crowd was so great that he left through the rear entrance and, making his way down Penny Street, walked to the beach and the small boat which took him and his companions out to the 'Victory'.

A few weeks later, his body was brought back to England, after his death in battle off Cape Trafalgar, and was interred in due course in St Paul's Cathedral in London. A column was erected on Portsdown Hill to mark his epic achievement in destroying the French fleet. For many years, the 'Victory' was moored in the harbour, a source of considerable interest to visitors and the centrepiece of hundreds of images of Portsmouth and its harbour. Finally, in 1922, she was towed to her last berth in the dockyard, where she is still the flagship of the Commander-in-chief, Naval Home Command and Portsmouth's most popular heritage attraction.

There were no crowds to bid farewell to the small convoy of ships - HMS 'Sirius', the brig 'Supply' and nine transports 'having on board a great number of convicts of both sexes' - which set sail from Spithead for New South Wales on 13 May 1787 to establish the first Australian penal colony, nor for the succession of convict fleets which were assembled in Portsmouth over the next seventy years. Thousands of men and women were sent out to Australia. It has been calculated that between 1800 and 1853, when the last convict vessel sailed for Australia, some 28,000 convicts were embarked for transportation at Portsmouth. Convicts became a common sight in the local community, living in hulks in the harbour until a convict prison was constructed in Portsea in 1851-3. The stronger and more able-bodied convicts were employed on public works. Beatrix Potter paid a brief visit to Portsmouth with her parents in 1884 and remarked on the numbers of convicts at work in the town supervised by warders on wooden platforms with guns.

When the 'First Fleet', as it was known subsequently, sailed to Australia in 1787, the two towns of Portsmouth and Portsea were fast reaching saturation point. Portsea Island was still very rural though. Travellers' accounts speak of good roads, well-cultivated land, 'shaded by noble oak' as one writer put it, scattered hamlets 'and here and there a house of entertainment' on the four-mile journey from the Guardhouse at Portsbridge to the Town Gate. There was also an extensive common field system, but, by the end of the 18th century, development was encroaching on these spaces.

The largely working-class district known in due course as Landport grew up to the east of the Portsea fortifications on either side of the London Road. One of the first residents of the neat rows of houses was John Dickens, a clerk in the dockyard pay office, who brought his wife, Elizabeth, to a modest house, now 393, Commercial

Road, in 1809. It was there, on 7 February 1812, that their first son, Charles, was born. Development spread north and east along existing lanes, to link up in due course with the villages and hamlets of Buckland, Fratton and Kingston.

The middle-class suburb of Southsea developed to the south of this area and to the east of the walls of the old town of Portsmouth. The first elegant terraces were laid out between 1809 and 1812 facing the fortifications. They were rapidly populated by the wealthier members of the local community and their families, many of them naval and military men, keen to escape the cramped and increasingly insanitary conditions of the old town. There were other attractions, too. Sea-bathing had been available since the mid-18th century. The old bathing house, Quebec House, a fine white clapboard building, still stands in Bath Square at the end of Point.

There were also bathing machines on the beaches, but the provision of recreational facilities overlooking the sea, where both local residents and visitors could walk, meet their friends and take the air, the Promenade, later the King's Rooms, launched Southsea both as a watering place and as a fashionable resort. Local builders were quick to seize the initiative, chief among them local

BATH SQUARE, ORIGINALLY BATHINGHOUSE SQUARE c1925 ZZZ04510 (From Gates)

architect, Thomas Ellis Owen. He was twice mayor in the mid 19th century and, for some years, there were few initiatives in the town with which he was not either intimately concerned or to which he was a party. Many of his fine stucco terraces and substantial villas still exist, in the vicinity of St Jude's Church, which he built to be a focal point of his development, and on the

A THOMAS ELLIS OWEN TERRACE ON SOUTH PARADE, SOUTHSEA 1890 22774

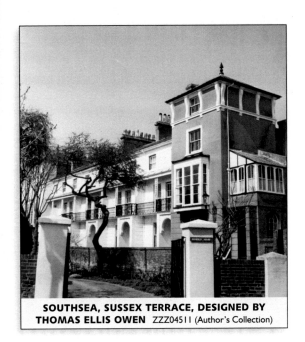

SOUTHSEA, SUSSEX TERRACE, DESIGNED BY THOMAS ELLIS OWEN ZZZ04511 (Author's Collection)

seafront near South Parade Pier.

It was owing to the initiative and energy of Thomas Ellis Owen that Southsea Common was drained and levelled, chiefly by convict labour, and that the Clarence Esplanade, named in honour of the Lieutenant Governor, Lord Frederick FitzClarence, was constructed along the seafront from the King's Rooms to Southsea Castle. The arrival of the railway opened up the resort to wider audiences and a great deal of local energy was put into improving Southsea's

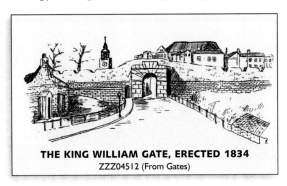

THE KING WILLIAM GATE, ERECTED 1834
ZZZ04512 (From Gates)

facilities in the late 19th and early 20th centuries. Piers, ornamental gardens, hotels and boarding houses followed in quick succession. A new gate was cut in the fortifications on the eastern side of the old town of Portsmouth in 1834 to allow the residents to access the new suburb and its attractions more easily. It was named King William Gate, in honour of the king who had been a midshipman in Portsmouth in his youth.

The old closed corporation was replaced in 1835 by an elected Town Council under the provisions of the Municipal Corporations Act. The first of several extensions to the borough boundaries which took place in the 19th century, took place now. The boundaries were extended to embrace the whole of the parishes of Portsmouth and Portsea. Only the northern part of the island was excluded, remaining for the moment part of the mainland parish of Wymering.

The population grew rapidly during the 19th century, more than doubling every fifty years from 32,166 in 1801 to 72,096 in 1851 and 190,281 in 1901. Such rapid growth brought increasing public health problems in the old towns and in Landport, culminating in the devastating outbreaks of cholera of 1848 and 1849. The report of the outbreaks by Robert Rawlinson, Superintending Inspector of the General Board of Health, did not make comfortable reading for either the Town Council or the Improvement Commissions of Portsmouth and Portsea, who were responsible for cleansing, paving and lighting. Rawlinson did not mince words. The outbreaks of cholera, fever and smallpox, prevalent at the same time, were due to, 'ill-paved and uncleansed streets, imperfect privy accommodation, crowded courts and houses, with large exposed middens and cesspools; and no adequate power for effective local government.'

The excess of disease, he said, was distinctly traceable to undrained and crowded districts, to deficient ventilation, to the absence of a full water-supply and of sewers and drains generally. It was a damning indictment of the failure of both the council and those in charge of cleansing, paving and lighting to get to grips with the needs of the burgeoning local population. Construction of a system of mains drainage commenced finally only in 1865.

Good communications with London, with the Admiralty and the War Office in particular, were always vital. One of the earliest turnpike trusts in the country - the Portsmouth to Sheet Turnpike Trust - was established in 1711. However, the Royal Mail still took the best part of a day to make the journey to London

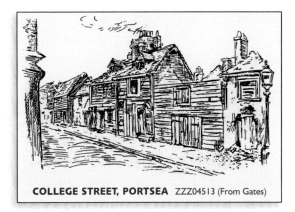

COLLEGE STREET, PORTSEA ZZZ04513 (From Gates)

The buildings here were regarded as typical of the poorest sorts of dwellings in Portsea

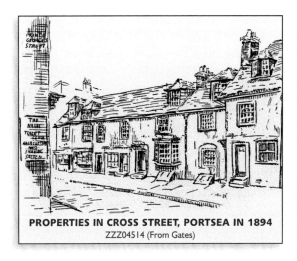

PROPERTIES IN CROSS STREET, PORTSEA IN 1894
ZZZ04514 (From Gates)

OLD HOUSES IN CROWN STREET, PORTSMOUTH
ZZZ04515 (From Gates)

These houses were demolished in 1906.

with coach and horses until the advent of the railway. The easiest way to move goods round the country until the railway came was by boat and, early in the 19th century, efforts were made to connect Portsmouth with London by canal. The Portsmouth and Arundel Canal opened in 1823. The promoters hoped that

naval and military traffic would use the canal as well as local traders, but it was never profitable. It was just as quick to send goods round the coast by sea from London. The route of the canal across Portsea Island to its basin in the vicinity of Arundel Street was filled in and the railway line was built over the stretch from Fratton Station to Portsmouth and Southsea Station.

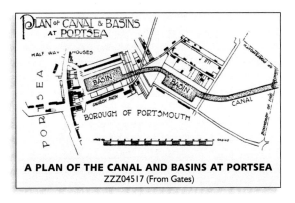

A PLAN OF THE CANAL AND BASINS AT PORTSEA
ZZZ04517 (From Gates)

The railway - the London, Brighton and South Coast Railway Company - did not, in fact, arrive in Portsmouth until 1847. The War Office had objected, for security reasons, for some years to breaching the defences at Hilsea to admit the railway onto Portsea Island. A direct route, through Guildford, Haslemere and Petersfield opened in 1859.

Other changes in travel and communications in the 19th century included the introduction of the first steam-packet service between Portsmouth and the Isle of Wight in 1817 and the opening of the Floating Bridge between Portsmouth and Gosport in 1840. A horse omnibus service was introduced in 1840 and the first tramway line in 1865.

Isaiah 43 - 2 - 3 -
Matthew 22 - 3 -

FORM

OF

PRAYER AND THANKSGIVING

TO

ALMIGHTY GOD,

TO BE USED

In all Churches and Chapels in England and Wales, on THURSDAY, the 15th day of November, being the Day appointed for a GENERAL THANKSGIVING to Almighty God:

To acknowledge His great Goodness and Mercy in removing from us that grievous Disease with which many Parts of this Kingdom have been lately visited.

LEGG, PORTSMOUTH.

1849.

A FORM OF PRAYER USED IN 1849 AT A SERVICE OF THANKSGIVING ZZZ04516 (Portsmouth Cathedral)

The service was for relief from the recent attack of cholera.

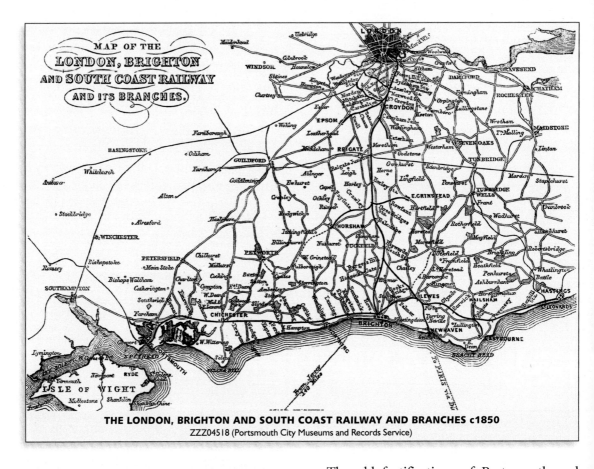

THE LONDON, BRIGHTON AND SOUTH COAST RAILWAY AND BRANCHES c1850
ZZZ04518 (Portsmouth City Museums and Records Service)

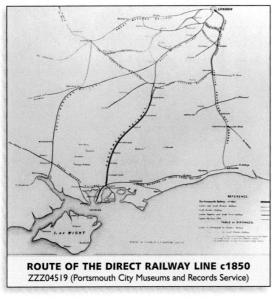

ROUTE OF THE DIRECT RAILWAY LINE c1850
ZZZ04519 (Portsmouth City Museums and Records Service)

The old fortifications of Portsmouth and Portsea were obsolete by the 1860s and were demolished between 1871 and 1878, except for the defences on the seaward side of Portsmouth, which were retained. The Mill Pond which separated the two towns was filled in at the same time. The land released was used for a public park, Victoria Park, playing fields for the naval and military, barracks, built for the most part by convict labour, and parade grounds. The City Museum and Records Office in Museum Road is housed today in the one remaining block of the Victoria and Clarence Barracks complex constructed on the former glacis to the east of the old town of Portsmouth.

THE FLOATING BRIDGE CROSSING TO GOSPORT 1898 42703

TRAMS AT CLARENCE PIER c1900 ZZZ04520 (Portsmouth City Museums and Records Service)

As development spread northwards along the London Road, out of the old towns and into Landport, so the commercial centre of the town shifted, too. A new town hall in Landport was mooted as early as 1879. The first town hall of which anything is known was built in the mid 16th century.

It stood in the middle of the High Street, roughly outside the parish church. It was rebuilt in the early 18th century on the same site, but replaced in the early 19th century by a building next door to the Dolphin. By the late 19th century the town aspired to a civic building more commensurate with

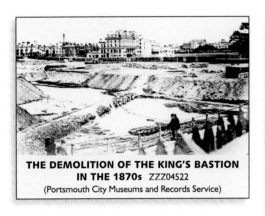

THE DEMOLITION OF THE KING'S BASTION IN THE 1870s ZZZ04522
(Portsmouth City Museums and Records Service)

SOUTHSEA, VICTORIA BARRACKS, PEMBROKE ROAD 1898 42698

SOUTHSEA, VICTORIA BARRACKS AT THE KING'S ROAD JUNCTION 1892 30008

REFERENCE.

1 Church of St. Thomas a Becket.
2 Garrison Church, old Domus Dei.
3 Old Mortar on Governor's Green.
4 "Royal George" Gun.
5 Old Fortifications remaining.
6 Old Fortifications remaining.
7 The Round Tower.
8 The Sally Port.
9 Old Semaphore Tower.
10 "Star & Garter" Hotel.
11 Old "Fountain" Hotel (now Soldiers Institute).
12 Old "Blue Posts" Inn.
13 The "George" Hotel.
14 The Museum.
15 Admiral Anson's House.
16 House where George Meredith was born.
17 House where the Duke of Buckingham was assassinated.
18 Admiral Lord Howe's House.
19 John Pound's House.
20 John Pound's Burial Place & Monument.
21 Chapel where John Wesley preached.
22 Old "Globe" Hotel—famous coaching ho.
23 Site of "Crown" Hotel.
24 Site of "Red Lion" Hotel.
25 Landport Gate.
26 The Quay Gate.
27 King James' Gate.
28 King William's Gate.
29 Admiral Palisser's House.
30 Kings Mill.
31 Mill Pond.
32 Mill Dam.
33 Where the Gibbet stood.
34 St. George's Church.
35 Site of "Three Tuns" Hotel
——— Line of Fortifications.

A PLAN OF OLD PORTSMOUTH 1925
ZZZ04523 (From Gates)

THE ROYAL DOCKYARD AND GARRISON TOWN

THE TOWN HALL AND THE MARKET HOUSE, ERECTED IN 1739 ZZZ04524 (From Gates)

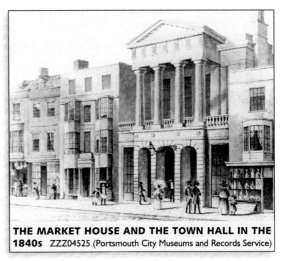

THE MARKET HOUSE AND THE TOWN HALL IN THE 1840s ZZZ04525 (Portsmouth City Museums and Records Service)

THE TOWN HALL AND TOWN HALL SQUARE 1892 30002

The Square is now Guildhall Square.

its dignity and status, and the new town hall, renamed the Guildhall when the town acquired city status in 1926, was opened in 1890 by Their Royal Highnesses The Prince and Princess of Wales.

79

In 1895, the borough boundaries were extended to include the Great Salterns, and in 1904, the whole island was incorporated into the borough. In the meantime, development, in the main of a residential nature, continued to spread north and east across Portsea Island. Clement Scott, who was holidaying on Hayling Island in 1897, summed up Portsmouth at the end of the 19th century: 'Municipally considered, I don't suppose that there are two smarter sea-coast places in the south than Southsea and Portsmouth. Everything for the public service, such as cabs and lighting and good roads and order, is admirably managed at both places; but I very much doubt if 'old salts' would recognise the Portsmouth of Charles Dickens and Captain Marryat…in the new, smart, red-bricked Portsmouth, with its magnificent barracks, park, and recreation grounds, its imposing town hall - one of the finest in the kingdom - in the Portsmouth up-to-date, which only requires a new railway station to make it perfect.'

The 'admirably managed' 'sea-coast place' of Southsea between 1890-1898 is seen in the views on these pages.

SOUTHSEA, DAGMAR TERRACE 1890 22764

SOUTHSEA, THE GROSVENOR HOTEL 1890 22772

SOUTHSEA, THE PROMENADE 1892 30021

SOUTHSEA, SOUTH PARADE PIER 1892 30019

THE ROYAL DOCKYARD AND GARRISON TOWN

SOUTHSEA, CLARENCE PIER 1892 30029

SOUTHSEA, THE BEACH 1892 30024

SOUTHSEA, THE SEA FRONT 1892 30018

SOUTHSEA, THE BEACH AND THE PIER 1898 42693

SOUTHSEA, THE WESTERN PARADE 1898 42690

SOUTHSEA, THE BEACH AND THE PIER 1898 42694

SOUTHSEA, THE BEACH 1898 42696

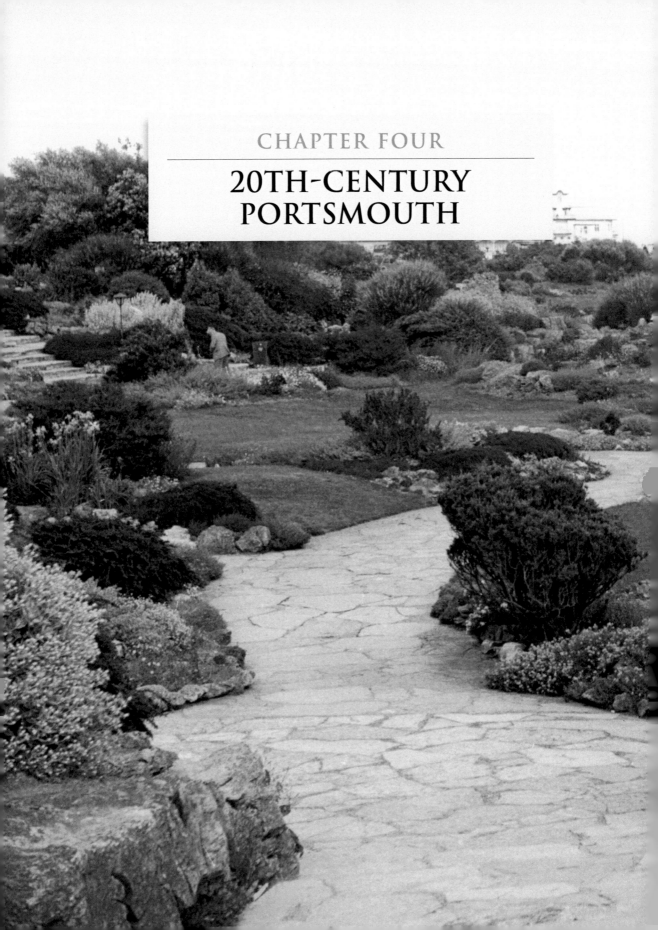

CHAPTER FOUR

20TH-CENTURY PORTSMOUTH

THE 'OLD SALTS' would certainly not have recognised Portsmouth at the end of the 20th century. The Portsmouth of Charles Dickens and Captain Marryat, author of Peter Simple, was destroyed by enemy bombing during the Second World War when, for the first time in the town's history, aside from French raids during the Hundred Years War, war came to Portsmouth. The physical face of the city changed beyond recognition in the brief 6-year period 1939-45, but other things changed during the 20th century as well - the number of people living in the city, the range and quality of the housing stock, the role of the dockyard and garrison, and the town's economic base. The seaside resort, modes of transport, the importance of the commercial docks, the religious life of the city, hospitals and education all changed. The change was dramatic and it was far-reaching. The 20th century was also the century when this city played possibly its most decisive role in the history of this country, supplying men and ships for two world wars.

THE BLUE POSTS HOTEL ZZZ04528 (From Gates)

The Blue Posts Hotel in Broad Street, immortalised by Captain Marryat, was built in 1613 and destroyed by fire in 1870.

THE DICKENS FAMILY IN PORTSMOUTH

Charles Dickens was born at 387, Mile End Terrace, Landport, now 393 Commercial Road. His improvident father, John, was a clerk in the Navy Pay Office on a salary of £100 a year. The annual rent of £35 for Mile End Terrace was really more than he could afford and by the time his second child, Charles, arrived, on 7 February 1812, the family's finances were in a parlous state. They removed first to a smaller, cheaper house in Hawke Street, Portsea, then to an even smaller property in Wish Street, Southsea. It was here that the family's second son, Alfred, was born on 28 March 1814. Sadly, the baby died six months later and shortly afterwards, the family moved away to London. Portsmouth features briefly in 'Nicholas Nickleby', but this is the only novel in which there is more than a passing reference to Dickens' birthplace. 393 Commercial Road is now the Dickens Birthplace Museum, decorated and furnished in the Regency style and with a small gallery of Dickens memorabilia.

The biggest change which took place, however, was in the number of people living in the city. By 1939, the population had risen to just over a quarter of a million. Such dramatic growth was no longer containable on Portsea Island itself and boundary extensions in 1904, 1920 and 1932 embraced, in due course, the northern parts of Portsea Island itself, Cosham, Paulsgrove and Wymering and, finally, Drayton and Portchester. New housing included the model homes of the Highbury Estate in Cosham, Wymering Garden City and the neat bungalows and semi-detached properties in Drayton, as well as handsome, detached properties along the Havant Road. Facilities in these new properties were wonderful compared with the small, overcrowded and dilapidated houses, often in narrow courtyards, which the occupants had left behind them in the older parts of the city. The new houses were described as 'heavenly' and like 'little palaces'. The houses on the Highbury estate were rated particularly highly, with their hot-water systems, tiled bathrooms and gas boilers in the kitchen.

Portsmouth acquired city status in 1926 and its prestige was enhanced even further

POST-WAR HOUSING 2005 P100717k (Sarah Quail)

A view of early 20th-century housing and post-Second World War housing development on the mainland.

THE ENTHRONEMENT OF THE FIRST BISHOP OF PORTSMOUTH, THE RT REV NEVILLE LOVETT 6 OCTOBER 1927 ZZZ04529 (Portsmouth Cathedral)

in 1928, when the title of Lord Mayor was conferred on its first citizen. Coincidentally, at this time, the Anglican diocese of Portsmouth was created out of the historic diocese of Winchester and the parish church of St Thomas's, Portsmouth was designated the pro-cathedral. Unusually, Portsmouth is now a two-cathedral city, the Roman Catholic Diocese of Portsmouth having been created in 1882.

THE CATHEDRAL EXTENSION ZZZ04531
(Portsmouth Cathedral)

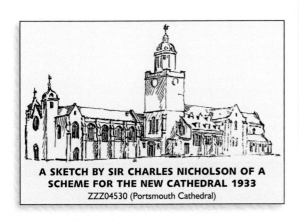

A SKETCH BY SIR CHARLES NICHOLSON OF A SCHEME FOR THE NEW CATHEDRAL 1933
ZZZ04530 (Portsmouth Cathedral)

The extension to Sir Charles Nicholson's scheme, abruptly abandoned in 1939, was designed by Michael Drury and completed in 1991.

CIVIC PLATE

Portsmouth possesses one of the most important collections of civic plate in the country, second only to Norwich's collection. The bulk of the collection was accumulated over a comparatively short period of 100 years, between the late 16th and late 17th centuries. It was then that the custom ended whereby newly-elected burgesses, prominent townsfolk or distinguished visitors gave pieces of plate to the town, despite the fact that, arguably, the town was entering its most prosperous period. The oldest piece is the silver-gilt Bodkin Cup, 1525. There is also an outstanding collection of late 16th-, and early 17th-century standing cups, including one, the Lee Cup, which has a partner in the Hermitage Museum in St Petersburg. The most notorious pieces are probably the Portsmouth Flagons, a magnificent pair of silver-gilt flagons, which were the gift of Louise de Querouaille, the French mistress of Charles II, who was created, for life, Baroness of Petersfield, Countess of Fareham and Duchess of Portsmouth in 1673. She was the mother of Charles Lennox, Duke of Richmond, whose descendants still live at nearby Goodwood.

Fact File

The City Motto

The city's motto, 'Heaven's Light our Guide', was registered in 1929. It was the motto of the Order of the Star of India. The star of the order has wavy rays of gold issuing from the centre in the style of the star on the arms of Portsmouth - a Muslim device. 'Heaven's Light our Guide' was also the motto of the old Indian troopships, which embarked their passengers at Portsmouth.

live in the city itself. The population fell to 233,545 in 1951. By 1991, it stood at 177,142. The figures have risen slightly over the last decade to 186,701 in 2001.

The fall was not a real decline in the local population, however. People relocated 'over the hill' to the former villages of Widley, Horndean, Waterlooville, Bedhampton, Portchester and Havant, which all grew significantly after the war. They moved to new estates built by the city council at Leigh Park, Wecock Farm and Crookhorn. However, despite the post-war relocation of a significant number of local people, Portsmouth was still a densely populated city. It is, in fact, the most densely populated area in the South East region, with 46 people per hectare. Before post-war relocation, it was even more crowded, particularly in the older areas of the city, built up between 1700 and 1850 and

The inexorable rise in the size of the local population was halted in 1939. The Second World War was a watershed. Thousands left the city to go to war, to escape the bombing or, quite simply, because their homes had been destroyed. Many never returned to condemned so roundly by Robert Rawlinson in his investigation into the cholera outbreaks of the mid 19th century.

The council's first slum clearance scheme in 1910 swept away some 200 slum properties behind The Hard in Portsea, which were replaced by an attractive street of model properties in Curzon Howe Road. The local authority built more houses after the First World War at Hilsea, Eastney and Wymering and blocks of flats in Portsea, but progress was slow. It was the devastation wrought by the bombing which enabled the city council to take more drastic action. A tenth of the city's housing stock - some 7,000 homes - had been destroyed, including most of the properties condemned before the war as unfit. Another tenth of the stock was severely damaged.

A structure plan was adopted in 1943. Satellite communities would be established on the mainland and the density of the population living on Portsea Island deliberately reduced to improve living conditions and the general quality of life. Land for new homes - some 1600 acres - was purchased on the mainland, including the Leigh Park Estate and, of the 22,000 local authority homes built between 1945 and 1974, nearly half were built at Leigh Park. Within the city boundaries, the Paulsgrove Housing Estate was the largest post-war housing development. Today, it is a substantial community in its own right with some exciting, developing infrastructure.

PREFABRICATED ACCOMMODATION (PREFABS) ON PORTSDOWN HILL c1955 P100003

ST MICHAEL'S CHURCH, PAULSGROVE 2005
P100705k (Sarah Quail)

The church has some important paintings by Hans Feibusch.

PAULSGROVE HOUSING OFFICE 2005
P100706k (Sarah Quail)

**PUBLIC ART, WYMERING COMMUNITY CENTRE
2005** P100707k (Sarah Quail)

On Portsea Island itself, the city council undertook a major programme of slum clearance and rebuilding which saw large areas in the centre of the city cleared and redeveloped. The break-up of long-established communities created its own problems, however. This, combined with fears that too many people, particularly the young, were moving out of the city, led to a change of policy. Demolition gave way to improvement, ie, the refurbishment of existing buildings. The first housing improvement grants were introduced in 1963 and the first comprehensive improvement area was in Stamshaw in 1971. As the naval and military presence has contracted in recent years, land has been released locally, much of which has been purchased by commercial developers for private housing. Hilsea Barracks, the Victoria Barracks and the Gunwharf have all been released and sold on for major commercial projects and, with controls introduced by central government in the 1980s on local authority spending, local authority house-building has ceased. Social housing projects are undertaken today by various housing associations operating in the city and surrounding area.

The dockyard and its attendant garrison continued to dominate the economic life of the city up to, and including, the Second World War. Some 1,200 ships were refitted during the First World War and the city raised several army battalions, in addition to its regular servicemen, Territorial Army members and naval recruits. 5,000 local men were killed, one in 50 of the population. W G Gates, the long-serving editor of the 'Evening News', recorded in 'Records of the Corporation' that the night of 3 June 1916 was probably the saddest in the history of the town. It was the evening that news arrived concerning the battle of Jutland. The German fleet was virtually destroyed, but at great cost to the British fleet. Of the 6,000 officers and men who lost their lives, the majority was attached to this port. It was said that there were 40 widows in one street. 'Sorrow hung like a pall over the city for weeks', said Gates, 'and the memory of that darkest hour is enshrined for all time on the walls of the cenotaph'.

Women took over many of the jobs which had been done locally by men before the war: on the trams, in the gasworks and the dockyard. The work in the dockyard was particularly hard and onerous and, initially, the women had to put up with considerable verbal and, in some cases, physical abuse from their male colleagues, but they certainly played their part in

convincing the Prime Minister, Asquith, by 1917, that it was impossible any longer to deny women's claims to the vote.

Fewer Portsmouth people were killed during the Second World War, despite such disasters as the sinking of the 'Royal Oak' and the 'Hood', although the telegram delivery boy could still recall, years after the tragedy, the trauma of delivering some 60 casualty telegrams in the North End area. War came to the city now. The only attempt to bomb the city in the First World War had failed when the Zeppelin's bombs fell short of their targets and into the harbour. There was no such reprieve now. Air raids killed 930 and badly injured some 1,216. The destruction was widespread. Over 6,500 properties were destroyed and a similar number badly damaged. They were mainly people's homes, but the main shopping centres of Commercial Road, Kings Road and Palmerston Road were hit as well. Properties destroyed in Kings Road and neighbouring Elm Grove included the draper's store where HG Wells worked as an assistant from 1881-3 and No 1 Bush Villas, where Arthur Conan Doyle set up his plate as a GP in 1882 and where he wrote the first Sherlock Holmes novel, 'A Study in Scarlet'. Other prominent buildings destroyed included the Guildhall, the Eye and Ear Hospital in Pembroke Road, the new Co-op Department Store in Fratton, schools, churches, including the historic Garrison Church, cinemas, the Hippodrome Theatre in Commercial Road and Clarence pier with its distinctive drum-shaped pavilion.

The worst raids and heaviest casualties

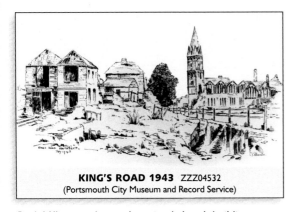

KING'S ROAD 1943 ZZZ04532
(Portsmouth City Museum and Record Service)

Bush Villas stood near the ruined church building.

occurred on 24 August 1940, 10-11 January 1941 and 10-11 March 1941. On the night of 10-11 January 1941, when the Guildhall was destroyed, 25,000 incendiary bombs fell on the city as well as high explosive (HE) bombs, which shattered the water mains and hindered the fire-fighting. Many accounts of the events of this night speak of the sheer frustration, of the pipes lying useless on the streets as the Guildhall blazed, the red, orange and yellow flames leaping skywards and illuminating the whole city, or so it seemed. The destruction of the Guildhall was a particular blow. The Lord Mayor, Sir Denis Daley, rallied his shattered fellow-citizens in the 'Evening News' that evening:

'At last, the blow has fallen. Our proud city has been hit and hit hard by the enemy. Our Guildhall and many of our cherished buildings now lie a heap of smoking ruins... We are bruised, but we are not daunted, and we are still as determined as ever to stand side by side with other cities who have felt the blast of the enemy, and we shall, with them, persevere with an unflagging spirit towards a conclusive and decisive 'Victory'.

Thousands of local children were evacuated inland when war broke out and the schools were closed. Some schools had to be reopened when children began to come back during the 'Phoney War', but many children spent the war as evacuees, many in the Salisbury and Winchester areas. The other great exodus was made up of the people who trekked out of the city each evening to sleep.

Local businesses switched to wartime production. One corset firm now made waterproof cases for radios. With dressmakers and seamstresses, staymakers had accounted for between 21% and 33% of the town's industrial employment between 1841 and 1901. A large female labour force was always available: the wives of dockyard workers, naval men and soldiers on foreign service. In 1901, there were still fifteen corset factories in Portsmouth, employing over 2,000 people, mostly women, but, by the end of the century, the trade had all but disappeared. Other local businesses which switched to wartime needs included White and Newton, the furniture manufacturers, who made parts for Airspeed. Once again, women took over men's jobs. They worked as riveters, welders and electricians in the dockyard and they built aircraft at Airspeed.

As for the dockyard itself, during the 20th century, the historic pattern of expansion and contraction, as the demands made on the work force fluctuated, continued throughout the century. The armaments race with Germany in the years before the outbreak of war in 1914 saw the dockyard workforce almost double from 8,000 men at the turn of the century to 15,000 in 1914, rising to 23,000 by 1917. Lay-offs followed and the 1920s saw not only significant reductions in the number of dockyard employees, which fell back to pre-war levels of roughly 12,000, but similar reductions in ship construction. The work force did not expand again until the mid 1930s, when fear of war once more with Germany launched a rearmament policy again. By 1939, the number of dockyard employees was back to pre-First World War levels, but by 1945 was at an all-time high of 25,000. Some 2,500 ships were refitted and repaired during the Second World War, rising to a peak of activity in the frenetic weeks and months before D-day on 6 June 1944.

PORTSMOUTH AND D-DAY

From mid August 1943, access to the seafront was restricted unless you had a special permit or temporary pass and from 1 April 1944, a ban was introduced affecting a belt ten miles deep, from the Wash to Lands End. You could neither enter nor leave these areas and a close watch was kept on railway and bus stations to ensure that there was compliance with these instructions. What few people knew was the fact that the approach of D-Day was gathering momentum. Since 1943, troops had been in training for the invasion of Europe. One of the biggest exercises took place locally in May 1944, when British and Canadian troops 'invaded' Littlehampton, Bracklesham Bay and Hayling Island. That something was afoot was clear from the numbers of vehicles and tanks heading south, and the work underway to establish inland repair bases and build and improve berthing facilities and slipways. By the time the invasion began, there was accommodation locally for 3,000 landing craft, billets for 29,000 personnel and 172,000 square feet of storage space. During the first month after the invasion, 207,000 men - and some women, mainly nursing sisters - and 37,000 vehicles were embarked locally.

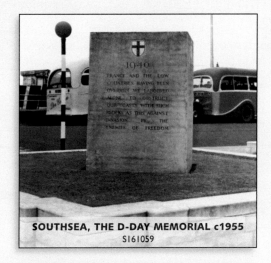

SOUTHSEA, THE D-DAY MEMORIAL c1955
S161059

THE WRECKED MULBERRY HARBOUR 2005
P100718k (Sarah Quail)

These 'floating harbours' were used to land troops in the Normandy landings.

The post-war rundown this time was not so precipitate, but it was, when it came, more far-reaching and it is clear, in retrospect, that the Second World War was a turning-point not only in the history of the dockyard but also for the development of the town.

Just as developments in military technology had dictated the reappraisal of the town's defences in 1860, so further changes now - in missiles and air power - led to significant reductions in the size of the Royal Navy and its ship-repair facilities. The numbers employed in the dockyard fell rapidly after 1960 and by 1981, there were only 8,000 working again in the dockyard. The Conservative government of the day took the decision in 1984 to reduce the status of the dockyard to that of a naval base, and its workforce to 3,000. Ironically, before the cuts could take effect, a task force had to be mobilised and dispatched to the Falklands. The ships were sent off in record time, but there was to be no going back on the decisions made already. The increasing privatisation of many services saw, finally, in 1998, the complete transfer of naval base services to civilian contractors - Fleet Services Ltd. The workforce was now reduced to 1500.

The garrison was redundant by the 1960s. In 1901, there were thousands of troops in the town to defend the dockyard. Huge barrack complexes to accommodate the men had developed since the early 18th century. The largest complexes lay between Museum Road and Pembroke Gardens and at Eastney. Troops were also garrisoned at Southsea Castle and at Point Barracks in Broad Street.

The garrison was disbanded formally in 1961 and the disposal of the barracks began. The city benefited considerably from the release of this land and other defence-related properties such as HMS 'Vernon', the former Gunwharf.

The lay-offs in the dockyard always led to serious unemployment. The council itself played an active role in attempting to relieve distress in the years immediately following the end of the First World War. An Unemployment Committee was established and, with the help of substantial government grants, a programme of significant public works was inaugurated, thus providing work for the unemployed. The esplanade was extended past the Marine Barracks at Eastney and other schemes included the construction of a new road from Portsbridge to Southwick Road, running to the west of Cosham High Street, and the construction of a new road from Portsbridge across the marshes to the west of Wymering. By 1921, the number unemployed had risen to 7,000. The problem was that there were few alternative sources of employment.

There was no serious commercial port. The Admiralty had always opposed efforts to expand such an enterprise. It feared that commercial shipping movements would interfere with naval operations - and this philosophy was adhered to well into the 20th century. Also, very little work in the dockyard had ever been sub-contracted out to independent workforces beyond the dockyard walls. So, if you did not work in the dockyard, you were employed in a very small enterprise in the town itself, serving the needs of the local domestic market. There were only a few exceptions to this rule. The Portsea Island Mutual Co-operative Society was established in 1873 and, from modest beginnings in rented premises in Charles Street, Landport, developed into an enterprise which still trades over much of southern England, and has an annual turnover of almost £200 million.

The brewing industry was another key player in the local economy, although, unlike the Co-op, there is no brewing presence in the city today. There were some fourteen breweries in the town in 1902. By 1914, they had been reduced to just four: Brickwoods, Longs, Portsmouth United Breweries and Youngs. But mergers, bomb damage, little investment and the need to compete increasingly in a national market in the post-war years led finally to the sale of the one remaining local brewing enterprise, Brickwoods and United, to Whitbread in 1971. Brewing ceased finally on their Portsea site in 1983. Some idea of the scale of the local brewing enterprise in the late 19th and early 20th century exists to this day in the many public houses still standing at street corners in the densely built parts of the town which survived the bombing. Brickwoods had a distinctive house style at one time, the work of local architect A E Cogswell. His pubs had black-and-white half-timbering on the upper floors and on the ground floors and the walls were often clad with lively, coloured, glazed tiling. Small spires and turrets sometimes adorned the roofs and made a distinctive contribution to streets lined otherwise only with small, terraced houses. Particularly good examples of Cogswell's work include the Swan in Guildhall Walk, the Mystery in Somerstown and the Seagull in Broad Street.

Fact File

'Brankesmere'

Sir John Brickwood, head of the Brickwoods Brewery, lived at 'Brankesmere', a house built for him in 1895 in Queen's Crescent, in the heart of Thomas Ellis Owen's Southsea, possibly to the designs of AE Cogswell. In fact, two Owen villas were demolished to make way for the Brickwood mansion. It has been described as 'complete artistic anarchy', resembling in many respects a number of Sir John's timbered public houses of the period. In its time, the house has been a hospital, during the First World War, a girls' school, police headquarters and local government offices. It has been returned recently to private ownership and is a private residence once again.

Historically, there were few alternatives to domestic service, shopwork or work as a dressmaker or seamstress for women in Portsmouth and wages were low as a result. It was this fact which attracted corset manufacturers to the town early in the 19th century. Between them, they employed, possibly, 2-3,000 women, many, initially, in their own homes and, later, on a factory basis. There were probably fifteen corset factories in Portsmouth at the beginning of the century, but only two by the end, owing chiefly to the decline in corset-wearing in the 1960s.

Two well-known, high-street names began life in Portsmouth, but they also moved on in the course of the century. Timothy Whites, retail chemists, was established in Portsea in 1848, and Gieves and Hawkes, tailors and naval outfitters, was founded in Portsmouth in 1785. They have a retail outlet on Gunwharf today but their shop on The Hard has closed and their flagship store is now at 1, Saville Row, London.

As for Airspeed, in 1940 a rival manufacturer, de Havilland, acquired a majority shareholding in the company. After the war, Airspeed made the Ambassador airliner and parts for de Havilland aircraft such as the Sea Vixen fighter and Comet airliner. De Havilland formally took over Airspeed in 1951 and, in 1968, the Airspeed Factory on the Airport site finally closed, production moving now to the north.

Diversification of the local economy was a developing issue throughout the 20th century. Considerable municipal effort went into developing Southsea as a holiday destination in the early years of the century. The Southsea and Portsmouth Entertainment Committee, a private body, was established in 1905 to develop the resort. Its assets were acquired by the local authority in 1920 and its newly-established Beach Committee set to work with enthusiasm. Southsea Common

was purchased from the War Department in 1922 and the paraphernalia of a self-respecting seaside town was soon acquired: bandstands, a rock garden, tea rooms and other refreshment facilities, beach tents, a children's paddling pool, a model railway, bowls pitches, tennis courts and seaside entertainment. Southsea's heyday as a seaside resort was in the 1930s and 1950s. Package tours and cheap flights to the sun took their toll of the traditional British seaside holiday though. However, tourism is still worth many millions to the city today.

SOUTHSEA, THE ANCHOR OF HMS 'VICTORY' c1955
S161042

THE CAMBER c1960 P100106

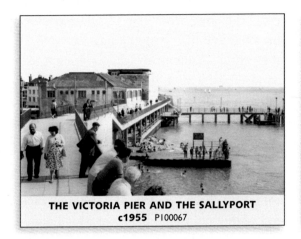

THE VICTORIA PIER AND THE SALLYPORT c1955 P100067

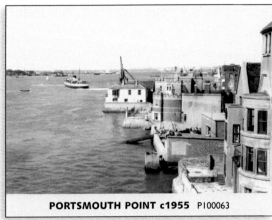

PORTSMOUTH POINT c1955 P100063

SOUTHSEA, THE ROCK GARDENS c1955 S161023

SOUTHSEA, THE BOWLING GREEN c1955 S161032

SOUTHSEA, THE CANOE LAKE c1955 S161049

SOUTHSEA, THE MINIATURE RAILWAY c1955 S161060

SOUTHSEA, THE PROMENADE c1955 S161025

HMS 'VICTORY' c1955 P100045

GUILDHALL SQUARE c1960 P100011

SOUTHSEA, A HOVERCRAFT c1965 S161123

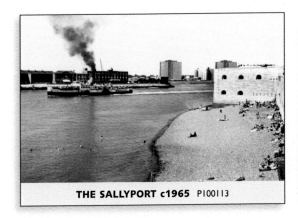

THE SALLYPORT c1965 P100113

THE HARBOUR c1965 P100014

Briefly, the advertising strategy changed, laying stress now not on the 'bucket and spade' charms of Southsea as a seaside resort but on the city's history and its naval and military heritage. Between them, local museums and heritage attractions, not least the historic ships in the naval base, the 'Mary Rose', HMS 'Victory' and 'Warrior', were attracting over half a million visits to the city by the end of the century and were factoring some £2.5 million into the local economy through a range of local providers of goods and services. The successful development of Port Solent in the 1980s as a marina as well as a leisure, retail and housing development, was the precursor of the later harbour regeneration schemes in the 1990s.

PORT SOLENT 2005 P100708k (Sarah Quail)

20TH-CENTURY PORTSMOUTH

The creation of the municipal airport in 1932 was another enterprising initiative, launched deliberately to create new opportunities for industry and development generally. Airspeed was encouraged to relocate here from York in 1933. Besides the success of its Oxford aircraft in training bombing crews, its 'Horsa' glider played a vital role carrying the advance guard of troops into Normandy the night before D-Day itself. The gliders were also used at Arnhem and, later, at the crossing of the Rhine. The airfield was used for commercial flights until 1973. The grass runways were too short, however, in wet conditions for commercially viable, ie bigger, planes and the airport closed. Much of the land was sold for private housing development.

Anchorage Park is now a well-established local community on the edge of the city, having easy access to main routes out of the city.

Industrial estates were created after 1945, when the city council acquired new planning powers. The first was opened in Fratton in 1947 and others followed in other parts of the city where suitable sites could be identified, such as Burrfields, Farlington and the Drayton Railway Triangle. Plastics and pharmaceuticals were manufactured and, increasingly, high-tech engineering parts and electronics, often for maritime or defence-related uses.

The city council was particularly proactive in encouraging large companies to come to the city in exchange for cheap rents and good infrastructure. As a result, IBM moved its British headquarters to Portsmouth, initially to premises designed by Foster Associates in Northern Road, Cosham in 1970-71 and subsequently to a reclaimed site in the north-east corner of the harbour, in buildings designed by Arup Associates. Zurich Insurance also moved to Portsmouth in the 1970s. Its elegant glass building towers over Victoria Park, reflecting the passing clouds. Defence-giant Marconi also established itself in the city, on the western perimeter of the old airport site.

The development of the city's commercial docks towards the end of the century has also contributed significantly to the regeneration of the local economy. The Camber was used by coastal traffic for much of the century, coal being the principal cargo. That trade has ceased altogether and today this harbour is used by the port's fleet of inshore fishing vessels. Flathouse was developed in the 1860s to take larger commercial vessels. It was expanded to form the Albert Johnson Quay, which opened in 1968, and Portsmouth became the largest fruit-importing port in Britain. More importantly, a decision was made shortly afterwards to expand facilities nearby and build new berths for large roll-on roll-off car ferries, thus opening up Portsmouth's commercial docks to lucrative cross-channel trade. Portsmouth's Continental Ferry Port opened in 1976 and ferry companies in Southampton were swift to move their operations from Southampton to Portsmouth. Easier access to and from the M27 and its spur, the M275, and a shorter channel-crossing, has made Portsmouth an attractive option for both holidaymakers and, increasingly, freight. The port has been extended four times since it opened and is second now only to Dover in the number of passengers and vehicles handled each year.

Public transport passed from private ownership to municipal control and back again in the course of the 20th century and valiant efforts have gone into persuading the public to forsake their cars for the bus. The city has very particular transport problems with road access. The M275 takes cars straight to the heart of the city, but only from the north, and the city centre and other pinchpoints suffer badly from traffic congestion, especially its effects on air quality. In the absence of any noticeable diminution in the numbers of cars coming into the city, considerable effort has been put into maximising the capacity of the city's road network. A new, light, rail system linking Fareham and Gosport to Portsmouth city centre through a tunnel beneath the harbour reached an advanced planning stage, but difficulties identifying adequate funding have made the implementation of this scheme in the foreseeable future extremely unlikely. Public antipathy, as well as funding issues, has also seen off a scheme to build an overhead tramway running north-south through the city.

The number of churches, chapels and mission halls in the city diminished in the course of the century. Church-building continued relatively unabated until the Second World War. The Six Churches Fund was launched in 1913 to raise funds for churches in areas not served by their own parish church. New churches were built in the northern and eastern parts of Portsmouth, including St Saviour's, Stamshaw, St John's, Rudmore and the Church of the Ascension, North End, and St Alban's and St Cuthbert's, Copnor. In 1927, Portsmouth's ancient parish church, St Thomas's, became the cathedral church of the new Anglican diocese and Neville Lovett its first bishop. There was some dissatisfaction at the time that St Thomas's was chosen over St Mary's, Portsea to be the cathedral church of the new diocese. But it was felt that being a cathedral church might disrupt the formidable parish ministry of St Mary's and its satellite mission churches in the Fratton area, which began under Edgar Jacob in the 1880s and continued with his successors, Cosmo Gordon Lang, Bernard Wilson and Cyril Garbett.

BRITTANY FERRIES' SHIP 'MONT ST MICHEL', COMING INTO HARBOUR 2005 P100709k (Sarah Quail)

A number of churches were destroyed or badly damaged during the Second World War and afterwards there was some rearrangement of parishes on Portsea Island. New church buildings, such as St Michael's, Paulsgrove and Paulsgrove Baptist Church, were erected on rising estates. Overall, it has been calculated that the numbers of places of worship declined from 91 at the beginning of the century to only 25 at its end. However, churches and chapels and other places of worship are still active forces in the local community. By the end of the century, between 2% and 3% of the population were still going to churches in the Anglican diocese, and some 40% of Roman Catholics went to Mass on Sundays. New ethnic groups have also brought their religions into the city, including Shia and Sunni Muslim families and Sikhs.

At the beginning of the century, most hospitals in the city were independent. The patient contributed to the cost of his or her treatment and the funding shortfall was met by donations and fundraising. There were medical insurance schemes, such as the Dockyard All-in Scheme, established in 1926, and extended subsequently to other workers in the city. A payment of 2d (1p) a week secured cover for hospital care for a whole family.

The oldest hospital was the Royal Portsmouth Hospital, founded in 1847 in Commercial Road on the site now occupied by Sainsburys. It was closed in 1978 and its activities transferred to Queen Alexandra Hospital. The other independent hospital was the Portsmouth and South Hants Eye and Ear Infirmary, which had opened in Pembroke Road in 1884. It was destroyed by enemy bombs in 1941 and finally relocated to Grove Road North. When it closed in 1969, its functions were transferred to Queen Alexandra Hospital.

Other local hospitals were publicly funded. St Mary's Hospital began life as the infirmary wing of the workhouse and it opened to the general public only in 1930. Initially, there was some reluctance locally to being

MILTONCROSS SCHOOL 2005 P100710k (Sarah Quail)

referred to St Mary's Hospital with its Poor Law connotations. The Infectious Diseases Hospital opposite St Mary's had opened in 1883, when isolation and rest was often the only treatment available for many serious illnesses. Developments in medical science have now removed the need for isolation hospitals and it was amalgamated in 1968 with St Mary's. Most of the site has been cleared now and a new school, Miltoncross, now occupies part of it. Locks Hospital for Smallpox and Langstone Hospital for the treatment of tuberculosis (TB) which replaced it in 1911 were both part of the Infectious Diseases Hospital. Langstone Hospital closed after the war, as treatment for TB improved dramatically with the discovery of penicillin, and better living standards were making the disease much rarer.

Two other hospitals were supported by ratepayers: St James's Hospital, opened originally in 1879 as the Borough of Portsmouth Lunatic Asylum, and a small maternity hospital opened in 1920 in Elm Grove, which moved to Trafalgar Place in 1927 and closed finally in 1938. Queen Alexandra Hospital was originally the local military hospital. It started admitting civilians only in 1941. However, by 1951, there were only 100 beds reserved for the military and this hospital is now the biggest hospital in South East Hampshire, with a greatly enhanced role scheduled for the 21st century, which will see more services transferred from hospitals in neighbouring districts to the new 'super-hospital'.

The 20th century saw secondary education provision consolidated in the city and the development of tertiary education, culminating in the polytechnic achieving University Status in 1992. By 1901, as well as the long-established Portsmouth Grammar School, endowed in 1732 by local alderman and garrison physician Dr William Smith, and a number of other private schools, including Portsmouth High School, which opened in 1882, there were 36 primary schools and one secondary school - for boys - managed by the School Board. The School Board was established in 1871. Portsmouth was, in fact, one of the first areas in Hampshire to set up such a board after the council had resolved unanimously to adopt the Elementary Education Act in 1870. It was disbanded in 1903 and its responsibilities transferred to the new local education authority (LEA). As the school-leaving age was raised successively to fourteen in 1918, to fifteen in 1944 and sixteen in 1973, so more secondary provision was made. There were four council-run secondary schools in the city before the Second World War. Today there are eleven. Modern, technical and grammar secondary schools were introduced after the war, with selection based on performance in examinations at approximately eleven years of age - the controversial '11+' examination. This system was abandoned in Portsmouth in 1975 when comprehensive education was introduced. There are now almost 70 state schools in the city, as well as a few grant-maintained and independent schools.

Towards the end of the century, subsidized

nursery school provision in the city increased significantly, driven by the government's determination to give every child that start in life which good nursery provision affords. The city has benefited from the developing tertiary and higher education agenda. A Technical Institute was established in Portsmouth in 1894. It became the Municipal College and moved into impressive new premises in 1908 behind the Guildhall, which it shared with the School of Art and the Central Library. A training college for female teachers was established in 1907 and also moved into the new building in 1908, where it stayed until relocated in 1939 in its entirety to its site at Milton, where a

THE OLD MUNICIPAL COLLEGE 2005
P10071 lk (Sarah Quail)

The College was built in 1908 and today is still part of the university's portfolio of buildings.

UNIVERSITY OF PORTSMOUTH LABORATORIES
2005 P100712k (Sarah Quail)

hostel had been established for its students in 1916. Highbury College was established in 1962 to deliver the Municipal College's non-advanced courses and in 1969, the main college, a highly respected regional college of technology, was designated the Portsmouth Polytechnic. Finally, it became the University of Portsmouth in 1992.

As the century came to an end, a major new initiative got underway - to regenerate those harbour areas now surplus to military and naval requirements - the regeneration of Portsmouth Harbour. Central to this initiative in Portsmouth itself was the sale of the Ministry of Defence building of the Gunwharf for development as a tourism, retail, leisure and housing complex by the Berkeley Group. Demolition of buildings on the site to make way for the redevelopment began in 1998.

The vision for the scheme was developed by a consortium of the local authorities bordering the harbour. The challenge was to regenerate a harbour area within a working commercial and naval port, to mix together business and leisure, heritage attractions, homes and shopping areas, linked by promenades and water buses. Over £90 million of investment was drawn together for this millennium project and a further £300 million private commercial investment for the two major waterfront sites, Gunwharf and the Gosport side of the harbour, the Royal Clarence Yard.

At the centre of the whole project, on Gunwharf, a landmark observation tower was planned to be built in the style of a spinnaker, thus echoing in its design the area's sea-going past, present - and future. There was also a further aim - to create the infrastructure for world-class maritime events such as the Tall Ships races and 'Round the World' yachting events, as well as for other major national and international events.

The 20th century was, without doubt, a period of quite remarkable change, which touched almost every aspect of local people's lives. These changes were accepted for the most part at the time, but there were regrets, not least for the loss of the close-knit pre-war communities, and new problems have taken the place of the old ones but, on the whole, our local communities are better off in many respects than they were at the beginning of the 20th century. The city has weathered the traumas of the Second World War, post-war reconstruction and the running down of the dockyard and, as the new century dawned with a dazzling display of fireworks, Portsmouth was well placed to take advantage of the opportunities beckoning.

UNIVERSITY OF PORTSMOUTH BUSINESS SCHOOL 2005
P100713k (Sarah Quail)

MILTON 2005 P100723k (Sarah Quail)

SOUTHSEA SEAFRONT, A HOVERCRAFT 2005
S161704k (Sarah Quail)

THE EMIGRANTS' STATUE 2005 P100720k (Sarah Quail)

The Emigrants' Statue was presented to the city on 27 August 2001 by members of the Pioneer Heritage Foundation, as a permanent legacy 'to the commitment of the Europeans who courageously left their native lands to create a new home in America'. Nearby is a plaque, unveiled on 26 April 1987, the 400th anniversary of the sailing, which records the fate of just such a group of early pioneers. The plaque records that 91 men, 17 women and 9 children left Portsmouth on 26 April 1587 as the second colony sent by Sir Walter Raleigh to the area called Virginia, now North Carolina. There, on Roanoke Island, they built the 'Cittie of Raliegh', the first English village in America. On 13 August 1587 they baptised the Indian Manteo, and on 18 August 1587 Virginia Dare was born, the first child of English parents born in the New World, and granddaughter of Governor John White. This colony, known as Raleigh's 'lost colony', disappeared between 1587 and 1590.

THE CITY has continued to strengthen its economic base. Gunwharf Quays opened in 2001. The attractive mix of waterfront drinking and dining, shopping and housing has injected a significant element of glamour into the city and visitor numbers have exceeded all expectations. It is estimated to have created over 2,400 full-time-equivalent jobs and provided household income to city residents of roughly £60 million per annum. When the Spinnaker Tower opens it is anticipated that another 460,000 people are likely to visit the tower in its first twelve months of operation.

THE SPINNAKER TOWER 2005 P100714k (Sarah Quail)

The Spinnaker Tower was designed by Headley Greentree and built by Mowlem.

GUNWHARF QUAYS

Historically, the Gunwharf - its popular name - was the arsenal in Portsmouth for cannon, mortars, bombs, gun carriages and balls 'of all dimensions'. The responsibility of the Board of Ordnance, whose origins can be traced back to the 15th century, it was situated just south of the dockyard and alongside the harbour. It was therefore well-placed to take ordnance off ships coming in for repairs or refits and equally to provide fresh supplies of weapons and ammunition when the ships returned to sea. It also supplied the weapons for the town's defences. Only small supplies of powder were kept there. The bulk was stored elsewhere - in the Square Tower from the early 17th century and at Priddy's Hard, on the Gosport side, from the early 1770s. The Old Ordnance Wharf, as it became known, was very cramped by the late 18th century and it had to be extended. Land was acquired south of the mill-pond channel and new storehouses were built here. This area was known as the New Ordnance Wharf. In 1811, work began on the Grand Storehouse, known today as the Vulcan Building, which is almost all that survives of the grand buildings which stood on this site.

There was an armoury on the Gunwharf for small arms. Old photographs show ships' guns placed in regular rows on the wharf and the balls formed into pyramids. At the beginning of the 19th century, there were elegant houses on the site for the officers of the yard and rows of trees which, it was claimed, 'have a very pleasing effect'. The site was badly damaged during the Second World War and many of its fine buildings destroyed. In its last years, as HMS 'Vernon', such 18th-century buildings as survived were largely hidden by unlovely sheds and unsympathetic modern office buildings.

The university is a similar success story. It has grown at an astonishing rate from the original 11,000 students in 1992 to 18,000 in the 2004-5 academic year. It has a huge effect today on the city's economy, population and nightlife. It is estimated that it pumps some £50 million into the city each year in wages, student spending and rent for accommodation.

Generally, the local economy is in good shape. The jobmarket is buoyant and although a recent announcement by IBM of a worldwide shake-up has alarmed workers at the company's site at North Harbour, it is thought that any cutbacks there are not likely to have a huge effect locally. There is, in fact, a very tangible 'feel-good' air in the city today, remarked upon particularly by people who have returned after some time away from Portsmouth. This optimism has undoubtedly been fuelled by the success of the local football team. Portsmouth Football Club won promotion to the Premiership in 2003 and has survived two seasons in the top flight.

An assessment of recent and current trends indicates that population growth rates by 2021 are likely to be in the region of 16%, which is higher than the estimated national and regional averages of 5% and 11% respectively.

Fact File
Vision of Britain

A new website - www.VisionofBritain. uk - has been developed at the University of Portsmouth by the Great Britain Historical Geographical Information System Project, which gives free access to historical data on Britain's towns, cities and landscapes. By simply entering a postcode or place name into the site's search engine, or clicking on a map, you can call up what is known about a particular area, what it used to be like and how it has changed. The data has been extracted from census statistics, maps, early gazetteers, and the observations of early travellers such as Daniel Defoe. The site is not just for academics; it has been designed to be easy to use by anyone who is interested in local history, including young people.

Fact File
Field Marshall Lord Montgomery of Alamein

A wartime hero, Lord Montgomery of Alamein was elected President of Portsmouth Football Club in 1944. He took a keen interest in the club's fortunes in the post-war period. Before the war, in 1937, he came to live briefly in Portsmouth on being given command of the 9th Infantry Brigade. He lived in Ravelin House, the house on the corner of the university's Ravelin Park, opposite the City Museum. A plaque on the side of the house now records his time there.

PORTSMOUTH FOOTBALL CLUB

The club was established on 5 April 1898, when six local businessmen bought five acres of land close to Goldsmith Avenue for £4,950 and formed Portsmouth Football Club. The first match was played against Reading at Fratton Park on 9 September 1899. The kit was salmon pink initially. It changed to white shirts and black shorts and socks in 1909 and in 1911 to the familiar royal blue shirts and white shorts. The club lost two FA cup finals in 1929 and 1934 before winning at long last in 1939, when they beat Wolves 4-1. Fixtures were suspended on the outbreak of war and the FA Cup was stowed away in the strongroom in the basement of the Guildhall until 1945. Portsmouth can therefore claim to have held the cup longer than any other football club. The glory days of the 1950s were followed by difficult years. There were peaks such as promotion to Division 1 in 1986, although relegation followed immediately afterwards. The club also made the FA Cup Semi-Final in the 1991-2 season, but lost the replay on penalties. The purchase of the club by Milan Mandaric during the 1998-9 season saved it from closure and marked a turnround in its fortunes. Promotion to the Premiership was secured in 2002-3 and work begins shortly on a new stadium at Fratton Park.

THE ENTRANCE TO PORTSMOUTH FOOTBALL CLUB, FRATTON PARK, FROGMORE ROAD 2005 P100721k (Sarah Quail)

The new preferred measure of wealth creation is Gross Value Added (GVA). Portsmouth's GVA per head is comfortably above the national average of 34%. Portsmouth has also seen the largest percentage increase in the Hampshire and Isle of Wight Region of registered businesses, although the rate of growth has slowed slightly, as has the rate of entrepreneurial activity, ie, new start-ups per 10,000 population.

But while new investment in the city, as with Gunwharf, has, in recent years, helped to transform the city's fortunes, and events such as the International Festival of the Sea and the D-Day 60 Commemorations, and yacht races such as the Global Challenge, have presented a new Portsmouth to international audiences, the city still has its problems. They are common to many major cities. While the GVA may be above the national average, gross household incomes within the city itself are below the regional average. Portsmouth has twice the national average of homelessness. Nearly 10% of housing stock is 'unfit' still and the gap in life expectancy between the richest and the poorest in the city is twelve years. Traffic congestion at key times of the day gives the city high, and rising, levels of air pollution. There is a widespread perception that away from Southsea seafront and the recent harbour developments, Portsmouth is neither attractive, clean nor particularly safe. Further, almost one third of secondary school pupils find school 'boring and irrelevant' and too many local people find difficulty reading, writing and doing simple mathematics.

When Lord Rogers and his Urban Task Force visited Portsmouth in March 1999, a local schoolgirl was asked to give her views on life in Portsmouth today and to say something about her hopes for the future. Among other things, she wrote that we needed to be proud of our city and the way it looked and that we should work together as a community to achieve our aims. 'We make our city what it is', she said.

Much has been done since 1999. A community strategy has been devised which is an ambitious plan to address a number of social and economic issues. It has been devised by the people of this city - a wide range of different organisations, groups and individuals - working together. The problems are not insoluble. A determined drive to raise achievement levels in local schools has seen Portsmouth achieve one of the fastest rates of improvement nationally at GCSE and a series of carefully planned community safety initiatives has seen reductions in vehicle crime, domestic burglary and anti-social behaviour. Job prospects have improved, too. A range of new jobsearch, training and capacity building initiatives has been launched, many financed through government Single Regeneration funding. Plans are afoot as well to redevelop the northern quarter of the city centre. The ill-fated 1960s concrete Tricorn Shopping Centre has been demolished to make way for a new mixed development of shops, houses and leisure facilities which will respect the historic street scene of this part of the city. A new John Lewis Department Store is the anchor store and more 'big names' are likely to be announced shortly. Meanwhile, considerable effort is being expended on developing niche shopping in Southsea's Palmerston Road, Osborne Road, Marmion Road and Albert Road. Plans are also beginning to be discussed for developing a cultural quarter in the Guildhall Square, an area where plans are far advanced for the construction of a new tertiary college in this part of the city.

Meanwhile, Gunwharf continues to develop. Its canal-side properties are almost complete and the final building programme is underway on the north-east part of the site where affordable housing is to be constructed as well as a residential tower. In the historic dockyard itself, exciting plans have been unveiled to utilise some of the vacated 18th-century buildings, notably the rope house and some of the storehouses, for hotel accommodation, apartments and other leisure uses. The city is also well-placed to benefit from developing links with mainland Europe. The sea, geography and, to a considerably lesser extent today, war, or rather, our defence legacy, still, between them, determine this city's life - and provide the catalysts for its future development.

THE GUILDHALL 2005 P100722k (Sarah Quail)

THE CAMBER 2005 P100715k (Sarah Quail)

THE MOSCOW STATE CIRCUS 2005
S161703k (Sarah Quail)

This took place on Southsea Common, on the Spring Bank Holiday, 2005

SUNSET OVER THE HARBOUR 2005
P100716k (Sarah Quail)

Fact File

'Pompey'

The origins - or etymology - of the nickname 'Pompey' are many and varied and, basically, you take your choice! It can mean the city itself or, if you are a football fan and a Portsmouth Football Club supporter, it means your team. The cry 'Play up, Pompey' echoes round Fratton Park and over much of the surrounding area when there is a home match. It is generally agreed. however, that the word is naval in origin. There are three possible theories which are just about possible. The first concerns the 80-gun French warship, the 'Pompee', which was captured in 1793. She fought with distinction at Algeciras in 1801 and finished her days as guardship in Portsmouth Harbour. She was also one of the ships caught up in the Spithead Mutiny of 1797. It has been suggested that her name became inextricably linked with that of the town in the turmoil at this time. Less likely, but certainly more amusing, is the story of the inebriated sailor, who fell asleep during a lecture on the history of the Roman Empire delivered by the redoubtable Miss Agnes Weston, who founded the Sailors' Rests. He awoke as she told her audience that the Roman General, Pompey, had been killed. 'Poor old Pompey', he is reported to have said. More plausible, however, is the story of some Portsmouth-based sailors, who, in 1781, scaled Pompey's pillar in Alexandria and, 98 feet up, toasted their achievement in punch. This feat earned them the nickname, 'the Pompey Boys'.

P100730k (Sarah Quail)

P100729k (Sarah Quail)

P100728k (Sarah Quail)

P100727k (Sarah Quail)

PORTSMOUTH HARBOUR –
THE 200TH ANNIVERSARY CELEBRATIONS OF THE BATTLE OF TRAFALGAR 2005

Horatio Nelson – Admiral Lord Nelson – is this country's greatest naval figure. He is also a Portsmouth hero. He was idolised by the local population and his ship, HMS 'Victory', is the star attraction in Portsmouth's historic dockyard. It was therefore entirely appropriate that one of the most spectacular maritime events of recent years took place in Portsmouth between 28 June and 3 July 2005 – a week of official celebrations and commemorations inspired by the bicentenary of the Battle of Trafalgar.

On 28 June the International Fleet Review took place in glorious sunshine punctuated only briefly by heavy showers, which did nothing to damp the enthusiasm of the crowds, which at their peak numbered 300,000 people. Some 60 Royal Navy ships were joined by a similar number of foreign warships and another 50 merchant ships. HM The Queen reviewed the assembled fleet anchored at Spithead from onboard ship with HRH the Duke of Edinburgh. There was an air display which included the Red Arrows in the late afternoon, and the day ended at dusk with a re-enactment of an 18th-century sea battle by a fleet of tall ships, and a dramatic firework display watched by crowds packing every available space on Southsea's beaches. The pyrotechnics were followed by the lighting up of the fleet.

P100726k (Sarah Quail)

The following day, in more sombre mood, the International Drumhead Ceremony took place in the shadow of the Naval War Memorial on Southsea Common. Veterans joined the present-day naval forces in a moving inter-denominational service to remember comrades from around the world who have died in maritime conflicts.

P100725k (Sarah Quail)

Finally, between 30 June and 3 July 2005, the Festival of the Sea returned to Portsmouth Naval Base. Europe's largest event of this sort celebrated almost every aspect of seagoing life. The general public were able to visit British and foreign naval ships alongside, both state-of-the-art warships as well as merchant ships and the elegant fleet of tall ships from around the world. There were combat displays, static displays, brass bands, live music and street entertainers. It was a glorious maritime extravaganza.

Nelson inspired the nation in his lifetime. 200 years on, this week of activities saluted his memory but also underscored the role this city played then, and continues to play now, as the home of the Royal Navy.

P100724k (Sarah Quail)

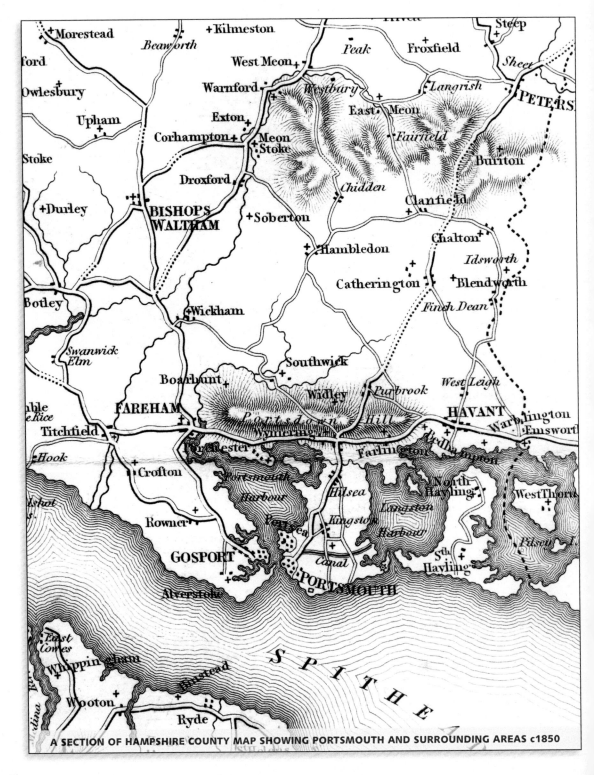

A SECTION OF HAMPSHIRE COUNTY MAP SHOWING PORTSMOUTH AND SURROUNDING AREAS c1850

ACKNOWLEDGEMENTS AND BIBLIOGRAPHY

ACKNOWLEDGEMENTS
I should like to thank the following individuals and organisations who have helped me in the preparation of this book: Paul Raymond and the staff of the Portsmouth City Museums and Records Service; Jackie Painting of Portsmouth Central Library; Dominic Fontana of the Geography Department of the University of Portsmouth; Butser Ancient Farm Experimental Archaeology Site; Richard Brooks, and my own family: my husband, Anthony Quail, and my son, Hugh Quail, who have helped me produce the photographs of today's city.

The majority of the images in this book belong to the Frith Archive. Those photographs which do not belong to Frith have been reproduced by kind permission of the Portsmouth City Museums and Records Service (PCMRS), Hampshire Records Office, Portsmouth Cathedral and Caen City Council. The line drawings have been reproduced from 'Portsmouth in the Past', by W G Gates. This is a limited edition of only 250 copies and is made up of topographical notes and sketches published originally in 1925 in the 'Hampshire Telegraph'.

SELECT BIBLIOGRAPHY
East, Robert (ed), Extracts from Records in the Possession of the Municipal Corporation of Portsmouth and from Other Documents relating thereto (1891)

The Victoria History of the County of Hampshire and the Isle of Wight, 5 vols (1900-12)

Gates, William G and successors (eds), City of Portsmouth. Records of the Corporation, 1835 - 1974, 7 vols (1928-83)

Gates, William G, Illustrated History of Portsmouth (1900)

The Late Archdeacon Wright, The Domus Dei or Royal Garrison Church, Portsmouth (no date)

Howell, Alexander N Y, Notes on the Topography of Portsmouth (1913)

Lilley, Henry T and Everitt, Alfred T, Portsmouth Parish Church (1921)

Lloyd, David W, Buildings of Portsmouth and its Environs (1974)

Portsmouth Papers, The (1967 to date)

Portsmouth Record Series, The (1971 to date)

Webb, John and others, Hampshire Studies (1981)

Webb, John, Quail, Sarah, Haskell, Patricia and Riley, Ray, The Spirit of Portsmouth, A History (1989)

Quail, Sarah, Southsea Past (2000)

Stedman, John (ed), Portsmouth in the Twentieth Century, A Photographic History (1999)

Stedman, John (ed), People of Portsmouth. The 20th Century in Their Own Words (2002)

FRITH PRODUCTS & SERVICES

Francis Frith would doubtless be pleased to know that the pioneering publishing venture he started in 1860 still continues today. Over a hundred and forty years later, The Francis Frith Collection continues in the same innovative tradition and is now one of the foremost publishers of vintage photographs in the world. Some of the current activities include:

INTERIOR DECORATION

Today Frith's photographs can be seen framed and as giant wall murals in thousands of pubs, restaurants, hotels, banks, retail stores and other public buildings throughout the country. In every case they enhance the unique local atmosphere of the places they depict and provide reminders of gentler days in an increasingly busy and frenetic world.

PRODUCT PROMOTIONS

Frith products are used by many major companies to promote the sales of their own products or to reinforce their own history and heritage. Frith promotions have been used by Hovis bread, Courage beers, Scots Porage Oats, Colman's mustard, Cadbury's foods, Mellow Birds coffee, Dunhill pipe tobacco, Guinness, and Bulmer's Cider.

GENEALOGY AND FAMILY HISTORY

As the interest in family history and roots grows world-wide, more and more people are turning to Frith's photographs of Great Britain for images of the towns, villages and streets where their ancestors lived; and, of course, photographs of the churches and chapels where their ancestors were christened, married and buried are an essential part of every genealogy tree and family album.

FRITH PRODUCTS

All Frith photographs are available Framed or just as Mounted Prints and unmounted versions. These may be ordered from the address below. Other products available are - Calendars, Jigsaws, Canvas Prints, Mugs, Tea Towels, Tableware and local and prestige books.

THE INTERNET

Over several hundred thousand Frith photographs can be viewed and purchased on the internet through the Frith websites!

For more detailed information on Frith products, look at
www.francisfrith.com

See the complete list of Frith Books at: www.francisfrith.com
This web site is regularly updated with the latest list of publications from The Francis Frith Collection. If you wish to buy books relating to another part of the country that your local bookshop does not stock, you may purchase on-line.

For further information, trade, or author enquiries please contact us at the address below:
The Francis Frith Collection, 19 Kingsmead Business Park, Gillingham, Dorset SP8 5FB.
Tel: +44 (0)1722 716 376   Email: sales@francisfrith.co.uk

See Frith products on the internet at www.francisfrith.com

FREE PRINT OF YOUR CHOICE
CHOOSE A PHOTOGRAPH FROM THIS BOOK

+ POSTAGE

Mounted Print

Overall size 14 x 11 inches (355 x 280mm)

TO RECEIVE YOUR FREE PRINT

Choose any Frith photograph in this book

Simply complete the Voucher opposite and return it with your payment (to cover postage and handling) and we will print the photograph of your choice in SEPIA (size 11 x 8 inches) and supply it in a cream mount ready to frame (overall size 14 x 11 inches).

Order additional Mounted Prints
at HALF PRICE - £19.00 each (normally £38.00)

If you would like to order more Frith prints from this book, possibly as gifts for friends and family, you can buy them at half price (with no additional postage costs).

Have your Mounted Prints framed

For an extra £20.00 per print you can have your mounted print(s) framed in an elegant polished wood and gilt moulding, overall size 16 x 13 inches (no additional postage required).

IMPORTANT!

❶ Please note: aerial photographs and photographs with a reference number starting with a "Z" are not Frith photographs and cannot be supplied under this offer.

❷ Offer valid for delivery to one UK address only.

❸ These special prices are only available if you use this form to order. You must use the ORIGINAL VOUCHER on this page (no copies permitted). We can only despatch to one UK address.

❹ This offer cannot be combined with any other offer.

As a customer your name & address will be stored by Frith but not sold or rented to third parties. Your data will be used for the purpose of this promotion only.

Send completed Voucher form to:

The Francis Frith Collection,
1 Chilmark Estate House, Chilmark,
Salisbury, Wiltshire SP3 5DU

Voucher for **FREE** and Reduced Price *Frith Prints*

Please do not photocopy this voucher. Only the original is valid, so please fill it in, cut it out and return it to us with your order.

Picture ref no	Page no	Qty	Mounted @ £19.00	Framed + £20.00	Total Cost £
		1	Free of charge*	£	£
			£19.00	£	£
			£19.00	£	£
			£19.00	£	£
			£19.00	£	£
			£19.00	£	£

Please allow 28 days for delivery. Offer available to one UK address only

* Post & handling £3.80

Total Order Cost £

Title of this book . . . .

I enclose a cheque/postal order for £ . . . .

made payable to 'The Francis Frith Collection'

OR please debit my Mastercard / Visa / Maestro card, details below

Card Number:

Issue No (Maestro only):   Valid from (Maestro):

Card Security Number: Expires:

Signature:

Name Mr/Mrs/Ms . . . .

Address . . . .

. . . .

. . . .

. . . . Postcode . . . .

Daytime Tel No . . . .

Email . . . .

Valid to 31/12/24

Free Print – see overleaf

Can you help us with information about any of the Frith photographs in this book?

We are gradually compiling an historical record for each of the photographs in the Frith archive. It is always fascinating to find out the names of the people shown in the pictures, as well as insights into the shops, buildings and other features depicted.

If you recognize anyone in the photographs in this book, or if you have information not already included in the author's caption, do let us know. We would love to hear from you, and will try to publish it in future books or articles.

An Invitation from The Francis Frith Collection to Share Your Memories

The 'Share Your Memories' feature of our website allows members of the public to add personal memories relating to the places featured in our photographs, or comment on others already added. Seeing a place from your past can rekindle forgotten or long held memories. Why not visit the website, find photographs of places you know well and add YOUR story for others to read and enjoy? We would love to hear from you!

www.francisfrith.com/memories

Our production team

Frith books are produced by a small dedicated team at offices near Salisbury. Most have worked with the Frith Collection for many years. All have in common one quality: they have a passion for the Frith Collection.

Frith Books and Gifts

We have a wide range of books and gifts available on our website utilising our photographic archive, many of which can be individually personalised.

www.francisfrith.com